Bio Davis, Bette   821 - 86
Dav
    This 'n that

DATE DUE

AP 23 '87	OC 17 '87	MR 10 '90	
AP 28 '87	NO 13 '87	JY 09 '90	
MY 20 '87	DE 15 '87	AG 14 '90	
JE 2 '87	MR 10 '88		
JE 19 '87	AP 20 '88		
JE 25 '87	MY 5 '8		
JY 16 '87	SE 29 '8		
AG 11 '87	DE 23 '88		
AG 19 '87	JY 29 '89		
SE 11 '87	NO 3 '89		
SE 19 '87	NO 11 '89		
Oct 9 '87	DE 1 '89		

THIS 'N THAT

Also by Bette Davis

THE LONELY LIFE

MOTHER GODDAM
(with Whitney Stine)

THIS 'N THAT

BETTE DAVIS

with Michael Herskowitz

G. P. PUTNAM'S SONS/NEW YORK

G. P. Putnam's Sons
Publishers Since 1838
200 Madison Avenue
New York, NY 10016

Except where otherwise noted, all photos are from the private
collections of Bette Davis and Christopher Nickens.

The author gratefully acknowledges permission from the following
sources to print material in their control:

Harcourt Brace Jovanovich, Inc. for the adaptation of "Little Word, Little
White Bird" in HONEY AND SALT, © 1963 by Carl Sandburg.
Mia Farrow for her letter to Bette Davis.
The Post-Telegram Newspapers for the review in the Bridgeport Sunday
Post "B.D. vs. Mommie Bette—Kiss-and-Tell Just Reads 'Dumb'" by
Joe Meyers, © 1985 by Post Publishing Co.
The Seattle Times for the review "Keep This 'Keeper' Out
of Here, Please" by Ed Baker, © 1985.

Designed by MaryJane DiMassi

Library of Congress Cataloging-in-Publication Data

Davis, Bette, date.
This 'n that.

1. Davis, Bette, date. 2. Moving-picture
actors and actresses—United States—Biography.
I. Herskowitz, Michael. II. Title. III. Title:
This and that.
PN2287.D32A3 1987   791.43'028'0924 [B]   86-22715
ISBN 0-399-13246-5

Printed in the United States of America
1 2 3 4 5 6 7 8 9 10

Dear Kath,

I dedicate this book to you, as, without your help in writing it, it might never have been finished, to say nothing about the fact that you helped me get through a great part of its contents. Who knows, your enjoyment working on my book might be a possibility of things to come in your life. Again my thanks.

Love,
Miss D.

CONTENTS

FOREWORD

THERE ARE MANY STORIES behind the writing of this book. Michael Herskowitz and I started working on it over five years ago. It was postponed twice. The first time, I took it away from our publisher because of artistic differences. At that point I decided to abandon the whole project. I was bored with books by Hollywood stars full of information that shouldn't be read by the world at large. I would not even consider writing that kind of book. Anyway, what did I have to say at this time in my life to warrant a book of any kind?

The second delay was due to the fact that I had a mastectomy and a stroke. During my convalescence, another publisher asked me to write a book and it occurred to me that maybe now I did have something to write about. Perhaps the story of my complete recovery from these illnesses would help others, particularly those weak and helpless from strokes, to believe in the possibility of overcoming the inevitable handicaps. So, write a book I did—*This 'n That* is it.

Upon its completion my publisher decided not to print my book. After the many months of work my assistant for seven years, Kathryn Sermak, and I had a great affection for and belief in the book, and we were devastated at the publisher's refusal.

Then I received another blow. I learned that my daughter B.D. Hyman had, without my knowledge, written a "not too nice" book about me. Interestingly enough, her publisher was the same one I had taken my book away from. In desperation I decided to advertise in *Publishers Weekly* that I had a book for sale. The result was the purchase of *This 'n That* by G. P. Putnam's Sons, who published my first book, *The Lonely Life*, years ago, and it was in my contract that the book would be published exactly as written. I was overjoyed.

By this time B.D.'s book, *My Mother's Keeper*, had come out. She wrote a letter to me in her book. I decided to write a letter to her in my book. This was the only change I made in *This 'n That* after reading her book.

I am still recovering from the fact that a child of mine would write about me behind my back, to say nothing about the kind of book it is. I will never recover as completely from B.D.'s book as I have from the stroke. They were both shattering experiences.

ONE

D DAY

O N June 9, 1983, at The New York Hospital, I had a mastectomy, followed nine days later by a stroke. My doctors felt there was slim chance of my making it. During my many sleepless nights in The New York Hospital, my uppermost thought was: Would I ever work again? Would I be able to return to my series, *Hotel*? Why had all this happened to me? It didn't seem fair. Over and over, lying there, I asked, will I ever be able to work again? Bette Davis and her career are one and the same thing. Acting had been my life. I wouldn't want to live if I could never act again.

I was panicked at the thought that I might be an invalid the rest of my life. I would be a burden to my children, to myself, to those who cared about me. Over and over people kept saying how strong I was. Of course I would get well. Of course I would work again. Especially encouraging was my secretary, Kathryn Sermak, who assured me daily, almost hourly, "We'll make it."

Kathryn lived in my hospital room with me all those weeks.

Many times I wasn't strong. At seventy-five I probably didn't have many more years to live anyway. What was the point of the long struggle ahead? To learn to walk again? To unknot my left hand so I could use it again? I gave up so often during those weeks.

During those sleepless nights lying there, I remembered, often with affection, so many people I had worked with . . . sometimes funny incidents, sometimes distressing. I thought particularly about *Dark Victory*, and I felt a bond with my character, Judith Traherne, who faced death, gallantly. I was trying to do the same. I remembered particularly often the costar I worked with the most, George Brent.

His performance as the doctor in *Dark Victory* was superb. It made the film a far better one than it would have been without him. I had fallen in love with George during the filming of *The Rich Are Always with Us*, many years ago. He, in turn, fell in love with the star, Ruth Chatterton. They were married after the completion of the film and eventually were divorced. George fell in love with me during the filming of *Dark Victory*. During our romance, he gave me a charm bracelet with the letters B-E-T-T-E in diamonds. I was a little less enchanted when he said, as I was oohing and aahing over it, "I'm glad you have such a short name."

George owned an airplane. When he had to play a part he didn't like, he would often buzz the studio in his plane, stopping all work and losing money for Warner Bros.

Many guilts of mine came back to me lying there. My third husband, William Grant Sherry, and I had a daughter. We called her B.D. for the initials of her first and middle names, Barbara Davis. I did not give her a father she could adore. Sherry—hot-tempered, brutal—must often have frightened her as he did me. I should never have married him, in case we did have a child. Even more thoughtless to marry Gary Merrill, without being sure he loved B.D. He was anything but fatherly to her. I accept guilt for choosing both of these men as B.D.'s father. I finally admitted to myself that this is why she married an older man at such a young age. She was looking for a father. Jeremy Hyman was thirty when they married; B.D. was sixteen. All these many thoughts kept going back and forth in my head.

Thank God, quite by accident, I discovered the lump in my breast when I did. Any further delay and I might have been riddled with cancer. I thanked God over and over as I lay there, that I had no cancer left after the surgery. I had been lucky in my life. Now I was lucky again.

So many things came to mind as I lay there all those weeks, some of them for no obvious reason. When you are ill and can't move around very much, it is unbelievable how your brain seems to work overtime. I remembered that during the filming of *The Private Lives of Elizabeth and Essex*, Charles Laughton came to visit us on the set. He had given a superb performance as Henry the Eighth, the father of Elizabeth. I said, "Hello, Daddy," and went over to where he was standing. I said, "I have my nerve playing Elizabeth at sixty years old—and I am only thirty." He said something I never forgot. "Never not dare to hang yourself"—meaning to accept challenges in the parts I chose; even though they might not be my best performances, I would learn to be a better actress for attempting them.

I often remembered my last few weeks in Hollywood, when I received many awards involving dinners. Many of my famous costars came to those dinners to honor me. I knew that I had a mastectomy ahead of me, and it seemed as I received each award that Hollywood, unknowingly, was saying good-bye to me, wanting me to know I would be missed.

I thought very often of the last film I worked on, *Right of Way*, with Jimmy Stewart. I thought about a speech in that film, unbelievably prophetic, considering what was happening to me. It was to our daughter, begging her to understand her father's and my determination to commit suicide.

> Would you like to know what it is we want to spare you from? The doctors describe it as a kind of starvation death. Except every cell in my body is a stomach. The pain will be immense. I'll lose all sense of who I am or what I am. [This is an exact description of me after the stroke.] I'll lose my insides and I'll lose my outsides. I'll be half my size and weight. Or smaller. A tiny figure lying on a rubber sheet in some hideous cinder-block building they call a hospital.

In the hospital, day by day I was losing weight. Just the mention of any kind of food made me sick to think about it. I knew if I couldn't overcome this loss of appetite I would never get well. The doctors had told me so, and finally they had to feed me intravenously. This was accomplished by putting tubes in the veins in one of my arms, which made it necessary for me to be attached to a large machine I called "Bertha," a name I've always disliked. Bertha stayed with me for weeks. I couldn't even lift my arm without being conscious of her. If I even tried to take a step out of bed, I had to pull Bertha along with me. She became a kind of jailer.

In *Right of Way* I also said to my daughter:

> I will be a figure you won't recognize. But also one you'll never forget. And inside that figure somewhere will be me. The Miniature Dwyer [my character's name] that will be remembered will be the one she never dreamt of. Or knew. Or cared to know. Or would let herself know.

Was that the way B.D. and my son, Michael, felt when they visited me after the stroke? Did I look so different and act so different that this is the mother they would remember, and not the mother they had always known? Since leaving the hospital Kathryn has told me many times about the way I looked. One of my oldest friends said, "The first time I saw you after the stroke, Bette Davis wasn't in that bed. She was gone." He was crying.

I remembered another speech Jimmy had in the picture. I now understood the meaning of it.

> It happens that I am tired. . . . I am tired of my feet and my nails and my hair and my shadow. It happens that I am tired of being a man. I'm tired of living. . . .

I could not have said it any better. That is how I felt after the stroke.

What fun Jimmy and I had working together. He called the hospital one day. I was so happy he cared enough to call me, to see how I was, whether I was recovering. His name in the film was Teddy. He gave me a teddy bear after the film, made of mink. It was in the hospital with me. The nurses were fascinated by a mink teddy bear, but more fascinated that Jimmy Stewart had given it to me.

In 1938 Brian Aherne and I played Emperor Maximilian and Empress Carlota in the film *Juarez* with Paul Muni. One night in the hospital we saw *Juarez* on TV. I made Kathryn laugh by telling her that one day during the filming, when I was off camera and Brian was on camera, after the take I said, "You should always wear a beard, Brian." I forgot how sensitive he was about his weak chin. He said, "You should always wear black hair." I was wearing a black wig as Carlota. Later, in Brian's autobiography, he said the only person who loved Bette Davis when she was a star was her mother. He had obviously not forgotten.

By living in my room during my stay in the hospital, Kathryn literally saved my life. It is important after a stroke not to argue with the patient. The patient can't take it. Kathryn also knew my reaction to being given orders. She constantly tried to explain to the nurses that they should do what I asked because they were exhausting me by not doing so. Doctors and nurses are apt to take it for granted that stroke victims are not "with it," that they misunderstand and don't remember what has been said to them. I was fortunate to have Kathryn in my room when doctors told me I was confused, and they denied that they'd said it. Kathryn was there to remind them that is what they said; and they didn't like it very much. I think they were the confused ones! Kathryn was not very popular with the doctors and nurses.

I realized, at some point during my stay in the hospital, that most doctors are convinced they are gods. Very often I felt that I knew more about my symptoms and my illness than they did.

My brain was in no way affected, nor was my speech.

One day in the hospital I remembered a party at my boss Jack Warner's house. I seldom went to large Hollywood parties. One of the guests at this one was that unique human being and gifted actress, Tallulah Bankhead. Most of the guests had left. I was standing at the bar when up swept Tallulah. I was a bit anxious about what her behavior would be. Rumor had it that she felt my character Margo Channing in *All About Eve* was a likeness of her and was furious that she had not been asked to play it. "Dah-ling," she said, "you've played all the parts I've played, and I was so much better." "I agree with you, Miss Bankhead," I said. She wafted quickly out of the room. She didn't get the fight she wanted. The films were *The Little Foxes*, *Jezebel* and *Dark Victory*.

I had lots of doctors; all of them came to see me each day, some two and three times. They would say to me, "Smile . . . squeeze my finger . . . look at my nose." Gawd, what noses! I was getting weaker each day from exhaustion. I finally convinced them that I did not require multiple daily visits. They ceased coming so often, thank God!

I also insisted they take me off so many drugs. I was woozy all the time. I had private-duty nurses around the clock. They were instructed, I presume by the doctors, to keep a record of everything I did, since they were constantly writing while in my room. They never took their eyes off of me. Every time I moved an arm, a leg, or even an eyelash, they made a note of it. I felt as if I were in prison! I wish I had kept a record on some of the nurses and given it to the hospital—they might never have worked again.

Often I sensed the joy that the nurses felt in telling "Bette Davis" what to do. Some victory! One nurse told me to say "please" when I asked her to do something. She should consider herself lucky to be in one piece today. Many times I had the impression I was a victim of something, rather than being ill. I did object when the night nurses snored and woke me up . . . at those prices! The morning I was scheduled to have my mastectomy, one-half hour before I went down to the operating room, the nurse on duty took my blood pressure and then said, "Your blood pressure is high. Are you nervous?" I said, "Nervous, I'm petrified!"

One morning a nurse came into my room and said, "Good morning, Mrs. Nixon." I smiled and said, "I am not Mrs. Nixon. Mrs. Nixon is in the room across the hall." As a dedicated Democrat, the last person I would want to be is Mrs. Nixon. However, having a surplus of flowers, I felt it would be nice to send her one of my bouquets. Kathryn asked one of her security men if he would please give it to her from me. Next morning the security man brought the flowers back to us, saying, "Mrs. Nixon thanks you but she is allergic to flowers."

I couldn't help but wonder, when Mr. Nixon was visiting her, if she had told him who the flowers were from. Maybe he was the one who was allergic to them.

The name Nixon made me remember many things about President Reagan. He was under contract to Warner Bros. at the same time I was. One of my vivid recollections was when he was the governor of California. A good-bye party was given for Jack Warner when he sold the studio to Eliot Hyman, the head of Seven Arts. All the contract players from the early years came to honor our former boss. Ronnie, one of the contract players, chose not to sit on the dais with the rest of us— Edward G. Robinson, Joan Blondell, Frank McHugh, Bogart, Bacall, many others. He decided to make an entrance as the governor of California. This necessitated our standing up for him as he entered. We all felt very silly getting to our feet for "little Ronnie Reagan." I would have loved to know what Jack Warner was thinking as he rose to his feet. I thought Ronnie used bad judgment that night in not forgetting his position as governor and being just an actor with the rest of us. Even later, another mark against him, I felt, had to do with Queen Elizabeth's visit to Hollywood. All orders for the dinner in her honor came from the Oval Office. Everything came from there except the occupant himself. No black-tie. We were furious— we felt like country bumpkins who didn't know better. All of us bought white gloves. No receiving line. It was a huge disappointment that Ronnie, as president, hadn't come to greet the queen in his own hometown. I was not the only one who felt this way.

The political history of President Reagan is an enigma to those of us who knew him then. He was a liberal Democrat for years. From the day he was hired as host for a TV series sponsored by General Electric, he became a staunch Republican. Prior to that Ronnie was president of the Screen Actors Guild and it was during his presidency that actors lost the battle to be paid residuals for reruns of all the many films we had made. This was unforgivable to all the members of the guild. Our films are shown over and over on TV, and now with the advent of video cassettes our loss is even greater. In light of today's witch hunts, when all political figures are targets, it is amazing that President Reagan, a former Hollywood actor, does not have something in his past to be revealed. It must mean that he was as dull as his first wife, Jane Wyman, said he was.

When the *National Enquirer* wrote of my illness, they were hideous enough to print my room number at The New York Hospital. The hospital and I were equally alarmed that some danger might come to me, since it would not be difficult for anyone to come into the hospital and find my room. From that day until the day I left, the hospital gave me round-the-clock security guards outside my door. I will always be grateful to them for that.

Toward the end of my stay, the doctors kept asking me when I was going to leave. They seemed to be trying to kick me out of my room, which I could not understand. Wasn't I paying my bill? My rather testy reply was, "I don't know, and I am the only one who will know when I am ready to leave."

I found out later that a very wealthy Greek shipbuilder named Stavros Niarchos had donated $10 million to the hospital, with the proviso that the room I was in and the room across the hall—Mrs. Nixon's—were to be available to him anytime he needed them for himself or whomever he designated. Niarchos, having learned that Dr. Behrman, head of dental surgery at The New York Hospital, was a great friend of mine, called him. In no uncertain terms, he told Dr. Behrman to get his "G—— d——ed actress friend," Bette Davis, out of the room she was in. He needed it for his son who had broken his jaw in Italy. Dr. Behrman is the one who later told me the story.

Every day I realized more and more that Kathryn had to have a break from the pressure of the situation she was in. Her concern for me, added to the uncomfortable living conditions, was beginning to take its toll. The only thing that really saved her life was the telephone. She talked very often to her beau in Paris. He gave her lots of encouragement. My worrying about her was not doing me any good either. I urged her to take a break and go and see her beau in Paris.

The instant Kath left my room for the airport, the atmosphere in my room changed. The nurses and doctors watched me even more than usual, and seemed to think that I would be unable to keep my sanity without Kath. I would never have given any of them the satisfaction that this was the case. I talked to myself many nights, saying, "Hang in there, Davis, hang in there." Every day for the six days Kath was away, a gardenia from her was brought to my room, each with a different note in her handwriting—these helped me so much in getting through the ordeal of "no Kath" each day. She also telephoned me from a pay phone in Brittany, as she was on an island in that area and the house where she was staying had no phone. It usually took two hours to get a call through to me. What a friend Kathryn was and still is. To say I missed her is the understatement of the year. But I made it, and Kath came back refreshed and able to tackle the hurdles that were still ahead of us!

TWO

WE'LL MAKE IT

THE DAY CAME WHEN I WAS READY to leave The New York Hospital. After nine weeks, the distance from there to the Lombardy Hotel, where I would begin my convalescence, was measured in more than city blocks. It was like moving to another orbit.

The morning of my departure made me think of the day I arrived at the hospital, wearing a beige suit, blue straw hat and high-heeled pumps. I left eight pounds lighter, in a green striped pantsuit and low-heeled shoes, and in a wheelchair. Some of the nurses and student doctors came to say good-bye. Among the many good wishes from my doctors was the hope that I would have no need to call them—for my sake if not for theirs. In the following weeks while we were at the Lombardy, I prided myself on not sending for any of them. They wound up calling me to see how I was.

Driving back to the hotel, seeing people on the streets again, seeing trees getting ready for fall, and inhaling fresh air, I marveled at how easily we take for granted nature's blessings. During those nine weeks I had so often wondered if I ever would be back in the outside world again. Everything seemed to be going by so fast. All of this brought tears of joy to Kathryn and me. We entered the hotel through the back door to avoid any possibility of photographers. The back door was where deliveries were made. I was being "delivered."

We had been given a suite of rooms new to us. After the dull greenness of the hospital room, it was a thrill to know we were once again in attractive, comfortable surroundings. Just to have nice walls to look at, room service, privacy and no doctors popping in on us unannounced was a joy. There was a terrace I knew I would enjoy in the weeks to come—To be able to be outside, probably potting plants and possibly getting a suntan.

During our stay at the Lombardy, every now and then I invited friends to come by. To one old and close friend I confided, "After a stroke you have a very 'short fuse' with people." My friend said, "Bette, you've always had a 'short fuse' with people. Don't blame it on your stroke."

I have been asked many times who was my favorite actor to work with. Without hesitating I always say Claude Rains. We worked together in three films, *Mr. Skeffington, Now, Voyager* and *Juarez*. Claude played the king of France in *Juarez*. I was very nervous the day I was to do my first scene with him because I had always been in awe of his great talent. The king of France wanted Maximilian and Carlota to step down from their positions in the government of Mexico. Carlota had come back to France to plead with the king not to do this to them. Claude was very harsh with me in his role as the king in the scene, I mistakenly thought that was how he felt about my performance. This, of course, was not so—He was only playing the part. Later in my career, actors were terrified of me in my different characters. They took it personally also. Richard Todd was cast as Raleigh in *The Virgin Queen*. For the first week he had great difficulty with his lines because of my appearance in the role of Elizabeth. One day, realizing this, I explained that underneath my appearance was a most sympathetic person who thoroughly approved of his performance as Raleigh. It helped him a lot during the entire film.

Claude Rains honored me very much by being my great friend eventually, and I his. He was married many times. One year he married twice. The wedding invitation he sent me to the second marriage said, "We printed this in the cellar." His second wife died that year of cancer. He never really recovered from her death. They loved each other very much. The real love of his life was his daughter, Jennifer, from his third marriage. I have seen her from time to time, and her likeness to her father is extraordinary. I will always miss Claude, as a friend and as a coworker.

The frustrations after a stroke are so great that they dwarf all other considerations. It took me three months to be able to use my left hand again. I exulted in small triumphs. I celebrated the day I could use a fork and knife. During B.D.'s visit while I was at the Lombardy, she offered to cut my meat for me. This made both of us laugh. I said, "I had to do this for you when you were little. Now you're doing it for me." Even though we were laughing, it really wasn't so funny to either of us. It also wasn't so funny when I couldn't tie a bow on my shoes or button up a blouse. When Kathryn helped me, I felt like a baby again. I hated it.

One day, while my friend and lawyer, Harold Schiff, was visiting, he blurted out, "Bette, you've got your legs back." For a long time my legs looked like sticks; no shape at all. At the hospital I had to use a walker, shuffling around like a mechanical toy.

In addition to daily therapy to help me learn to walk again and to straighten out my left hand, my doctors told me no smoking and no drinking. Me, who had always enjoyed the cocktail hour. As for smoking, only Sir Walter Raleigh is identified as closely with tobacco as I am. My doctor knew what he was asking of me. "This is an unfortunate time to ask you to give up things you have always enjoyed," he said. I did without them for a full month after I checked into the Lombardy. As a concession to my doctor, I switched to a low-tar filtered cigarette. At the cocktail hour, I was finally permitted a wine spritzer.

One night Kath and I saw Lauren Bacall's first film, with Humphrey Bogart, on television at the hotel. I remembered my first film with Bogart. It was a deadly thing called *Bad Sister*. We were both under contract to Universal and (no wonder, after seeing *Bad Sister*) we were both fired from the studio. There was a legend at that time that if you were fired from Universal, you would eventually make it to the top. Bogey and I most certainly lived up to that one. Interestingly enough we both became stars at another studio, Warner Bros. We worked together in *Marked Woman*, and in *The Petrified Forest* with Leslie Howard. This film made Bogey a star. He had played the same part on Broadway with Leslie Howard, who insisted that Bogey be in the film or he wouldn't do it himself. Bogey was also in *Dark Victory* with me.

Lauren Bacall was in love with Bogey even before she was a contract player at Warner Bros. Her first film with him was certainly a dream come true, and the fact that it all ended in marriage was remarkable.

Few people broke through Bogart's reserve. Not until he acquired the dissipated looks, the world-weary eyes, did his stardom become a permanent thing, and he was widely known as a pretty heavy drinker. The Bogarts and the Merrills were all at a party at Hedda Hopper's one night. Lauren was not the only one married to a lover of alcohol. I was married to Gary Merrill. Bogey and Gary had never met until that evening, and Lauren said, "God, wait till these two get together! We won't find them for weeks." Her prophecy did not come true, for which we were both thankful.

During my stay at the hospital, my surgeon, Dr. Shires, and the doctor who was in complete charge of my case, Dr. Tyberg, were the most sympathetic. At the Lombardy, they continued to be the most caring, calling often to see how I was doing. Dr. Tyberg is still my medical mainstay, even though I have returned to California.

After the *National Enquirer* ran the story of my illnesses and what hospital I was at, mail arrived from everywhere. Most of the people sent their wishes for my recovery. Many just wanted to know when, or if, I would return to my television series, *Hotel*.

My daily existence now revolved around a hotel, but not the one in the series. I had told Aaron Spelling, the series producer, that I would be able to return in January. This decision, while sincere, was motivated by my desire to go back to work, not by my opinion of the product. After I appeared in the pilot, it was never the show I imagined it could be or would have been, I think, had I continued in it. After watching the episodes each week I thought that *Hotel* should have been called *Brothel*—there was never an episode without someone hopping in and out of someone else's bed.

Mr. Spelling kept sending me scripts for my future episodes in *Hotel*, each worse than the last. In the first episode after my return I was to cure Anne Baxter, who had taken my character's place during my absence, of drug addiction. In another, I was to be taken hostage by terrorists. Had a suitable script arrived, I would definitely have returned to the series. I waited for an announcement to be made that I would not be back. When none came, I begged Aaron Spelling to issue a statement that I was not returning. I felt this was only fair to those who would tune in week after week expecting to see me.

Whatever my ups and downs, Kathryn was there to assure me over and over, saying, "We'll make it." I now weighed only ninety-two pounds. The summer clothes I brought to New York not only didn't fit, they were also out of season. Kathryn brought me some new clothes with as few buttons as possible, and with sleeves I could get in and out of by myself.

Mia Farrow telephoned me one day at the hotel. In 1958 I was in the film *John Paul Jones*, directed by her father, John Farrow, in Madrid. B.D. and Mia were both about twelve years old and became close friends. Mia went with us on all our sightseeing trips—to Toledo, to museums, everywhere. Mia became a successful star in the series *Peyton Place*. While I was filming *Hush . . . Hush, Sweet Charlotte* she came to visit me on the set. She stood there looking at me. I didn't recognize her. Realizing this, she said, "It's Mia Farrow." We hugged. She had become a very pretty grown-up young lady.

Mia and I saw each other from time to time after that when we were in the East. During the period that she and Frank Sinatra were in love with each other and everyone felt they would marry, she came to me for advice. She told me that he said if he married her she would have to give up her career. I begged Mia not to agree to this. They did marry, and eventually were divorced. Since that time Mia has given some superb performances. When we were in Egypt making *Death on the Nile*, she gave another excellent performance. It was fun to work with her, and Mia was a sort of daughter to me.

My son, Michael, busy as he was with his law practice, found time to visit me often while I was at the Lombardy. He was overjoyed at my progress each time he came. I was again looking and acting like the mother he had known all through the years.

My nights were long and sometimes sleepless. My temper was short, not necessarily a bad sign. No one at the hospital realized that this was a sign of my improvement. When I raised my voice, they thought I needed a sedative but Kathryn was thrilled I was behaving this way. She knew it was a sure sign I was getting better.

One night during our stay at the hotel, Kath and I saw *Jezebel* on television. It brought back many memories, mostly having to do with William Wyler, the director, and Henry Fonda, my costar. I first met William Wyler, who eventually became my favorite director, when we were both under contract to Universal. I was to be tested for the part of the young girl in *Heart and Hand,* starring Walter Huston. It would have been a terrific boost to my film career if I had made a good test. For the test the wardrobe department gave me a dress that was much too low in front. I was embarrassed by it. As I walked on the soundstage I heard Mr. Wyler say to someone on the set, "What do you think of these dames who show their chest and think they'll get jobs!" Quite understandably this destroyed me; my performance on the test was very bad. Driving home that day I vowed that someday I would get even with that horrible little man. Through the years I never gave up hoping that one day I would have the opportunity for revenge.

Mr. Wyler's career reached great heights in later years, and so did mine. My boss, Hal Wallis, sent for me one day and said he had some good news. My director for *Jezebel* would be William Wyler. The moment had come. I was then in a position to accept or reject Mr. Wyler as director of the film. I could not wait to meet with him about his plans for the film, and eventually I was asked to his office to discuss them. After the usual how-do-you-dos, I waited a bit before I launched into the story of our first meeting. Finally I said, "I have a story to tell you, Mr. Wyler. We have met before," and on and on I went. At the end there was dead silence. Then he said, "I'm nicer now." With that he robbed me of my revenge. What a letdown!

Being directed by Wyler was a challenge, a joy, and an education. He was always demanding and often rude. He once said loudly, "If you don't stop moving your head, I'll put a chain around your neck." After each take he printed, he never told us if it was what he wanted. A few days into the shooting of *Jezebel,* I explained to him that I was the kind of actress who had to know if she was giving the director what he wanted. He smiled and said nothing, but for the rest of the day, after each take he printed, he clapped his hands and said, "Mah-velous, Miss Davis, mah-velous." I laughed and asked him to return to the earlier way.

Fonda and I had met many years before at the Cape Playhouse on Cape Cod. I was madly in love with him; he didn't know I existed. This was the second time we had worked together, both on Warner films. The first, *That Certain Woman*, was not a favorite for either of us. We were behind schedule on *Jezebel*. According to Fonda's contract, he could be with his wife when their first child was born. As a result, all my closeups in scenes with him were played to a strange voice and a stick with a round piece of wood with a face painted on it. I have long forgiven him for this, since that baby turned out to be Jane Fonda.

From the day I left the hospital, one dread hung over me. How would I manage the long airplane trip home to California? I was afraid, of course, that I might have another stroke in front of the other passengers. It was an even more terrifying prospect for Kathryn who would have been as helpless as I if anything had gone wrong at thirty thousand feet.

I asked Dr. Shires if I could take my favorite intern, Dr. Paul, who had been kind and caring to me at the hospital. Dr. Shires said yes, and we were grateful for Dr. Paul's presence. As it turned out, the plane trip did not faze me at all.

It was almost Thanksgiving and we were going home. I did not know then that my convalescence would last for more than a year. During my fifty-three-year career, I had never gone so long without working. For all these months I was well aware that my final hurdle would be my ability to continue my career.

Since it is by now obvious what a large part Kathryn played in what has been written about so far, I thought it would be of interest to the reader to know about *her* life, and how she came into mine. It was during our stay at the Lombardy that we began working on this book.

Kathryn was the middle child, with three sisters and one

brother. They were brought up in a strict Catholic home where they lived by their father's rules and his European values. They all worked to earn whatever pocket money they needed. Kathryn hoarded every dime against the day she could travel beyond the city limits of San Bernardino, California, her hometown. She washed dishes to pay for classes one summer in Hawaii, and worked as an au pair girl to finance a year of studies in Paris. Scholarships helped pay most of her tuition, along with part-time work.

Kathryn thought she wanted to be a doctor of clinical psychology, and she had the opportunity to study under Carl Rogers and Jane Goodall. She graduated from the University of Southern California, having started the first work-study program in Spain. Then one day she realized she had chosen psychology for the wrong reasons. She often pictured herself in a Beverly Hills office with DR. KATHRYN SERMAK on the door, later inventing some new theory of psychology. She thought this career would bring her security, identity, wealth and fame. Kathryn also wanted to impress her father. But she finally realized that psychology was not the field she wanted to spend her life in and gave it up.

The next chapter has been written by Kath herself. It contains her first impressions of me and her subsequent feelings after living and working with me for seven years.

THREE

AS KATH SEES ME

M Y FIRST IMPRESSION OF MISS D. was how strong a handshake she had for a woman. I was wearing a ring and it left an imprint on my fingers. I later found out Miss D. judged people by their handshakes. To her, a firm one was the sign of a worthwhile person. Later on, she had me practice a firm handshake with her.

Miss D. was interviewing people in hopes of finding someone to accompany her to England, where she was to make a film. She gave me the job after an interview that could not have lasted much longer than seven minutes. She asked me what my birth sign was (Libra) and could I boil an egg (yes). Actually, the second answer was only partly true. In our home all we knew were hard-boiled eggs. I thought you always cooked them half an hour.

In the beginning of the interview, I explained that I knew nothing about the film industry, having been brought up in a family in which the work ethic was solidly entrenched and motion pictures were considered luxuries. "Don't worry," Miss D. said, "I will tell you whatever you need to know." Then, to my amazement, she told me I had the job and we would leave for England in a few weeks. Miss D. later told me her quick decision to give me the job was based on a hunch she had about me. She also would often say, "My hunch was certainly right."

From the patio where we sat, I could see her two Oscars on a shelf, among many other awards. Walking through Miss D.'s apartment was like a trip through a museum.

If I think back now to that day in June 1979, it is hard to imagine how she could have found anyone less aware of the career of Bette Davis. This no doubt worked to my advantage. It also reflected her lack of vanity, and her desire to reach for what passed as normal, in a world that was so seldom normal.

I was not yet twenty-three. I learned much later—it was two years before the subject came up—that the employment agency had lied about my age. Had she known how young I was, she might never have hired me.

In the few weeks I had left to organize myself, I read her autobiography, *The Lonely Life.* On the day we left for England, after I had spent my first night in her apartment, I made an entry in a notebook I kept (to call it a diary is to give it more shape than it had):

"She is divine. Last night she cooked me a marvelous dinner of Cornish hen, squash with green peas. She is delightful and charming and has a heart. A good person, I can tell. . . . Her home is beautiful, filled with warmth and loving pieces from parts of her life. . . ."

I felt amazed and a little guilty at letting her cook dinner for me. I thought, "I should be doing this for her." I began to wonder what would happen when she found out I knew very little about cooking (including eggs, as she later found out).

I had never met anyone so energetic. It was impossible for me to think of her as being in her seventies because I found it hard to keep up with her. In spite of the warning I had given her at our interview, I don't think she ever realized how little I knew about her, motion pictures or life. I had graduated from college resisting the pressure that every student feels, at twenty or twenty-one, to map out his or her entire life.

The name of the film we made in England was *Watcher in the Woods*. In it Miss D. played the "watcher," but as it turned out, we were both playing the same part. I was at my new job, in the woods, watching her every minute. It was not a taxing part for Miss D., and it was a good way to introduce me to working with her. During the first days on the set she told me to stay nearby and she would explain things. I did not mix with the other people who were part of the support system that develops on the set of any film, and one and all probably thought I was cold and aloof because I didn't lounge around and gossip. I behaved as Miss D. did. She set the tone not just for me, but for the others on this and each new film we did. The production would become more organized as cast and crew followed her example. She always arrived on the set dressed impeccably, and soon everyone else did too. She inspired pride in everyone. She always stood up for the cast and crew if they ran into trouble with the production office.

When we returned to California, Miss D. was going to make a special for television called *White Mama*. Peggy Shannon, her longtime hairdresser, who had not been well enough to make the trip to London, was still not well enough to do her hair for *White Mama*. This was a lucky break for me, because Miss D., as usual, needed someone on the set to help her with many things. She asked me to move into her apartment, where I lived for seven years, learning many other things. One of them was how to cook. No more hard-boiled eggs. From then on she referred to me as her secretary.

Some people are born to be teachers and some are born to be students. Miss D. is, was, and always will be a teacher. This I know: I learned from her every day. It was easy to work for

Miss D. because she was always decisive: This is right, that is wrong. She always pays a compliment when you do a job well. If you make a mistake she corrects you. Just don't make the same mistake again.

The first time I really became aware of the extent of Miss D.'s fame was when she was honored with a festival of her films at the Los Angeles County Museum. I had been on sets with her and had been enlightened by her fan mail, but I had never attended a public function with her. I was in the wings when she walked onstage, and more than a thousand people rose and gave her a standing ovation. I'm sure my jaw dropped. I saw Miss D. in a different light: That's the woman I work for, the one with the pretty hats, who likes to keep busy around the house, cooking, setting the table, arranging the flowers, dusting the furniture she has collected over a lifetime and has moved across the country more than once. I got chills watching her. There is something about Miss D. when she steps onstage—almost a physical transformation. She seemed to grow larger in front of my eyes. It was like watching one of those body-building contests, where a contestant looks fairly average one moment, enlarged the next.

I was amazed at how bright and quick she was, tossing off answers to questions from the audience with complete spontaneity. One woman asked if she was disappointed that she was not considered one of the "glamour girl" movie stars. She responded quickly: "Wouldn't it be a rather meager ambition if that was all one strived for?" The audience roared.

A few minutes later, a man gave Miss D. a quote from one of her films and asked if she remembered it. Miss D. thought for a moment and then said, "It is from *In This Our Life*, in which I worked with a promising young black actor," and added, "What a splendid actor he has become." The man who asked the question was that youngster, now forty years older. His name was Ernest Anderson.

With all the films she had made, I was astonished that she

could reach so far back and remember one line in particular. One lady asked if she would tell some "juicy" stories about actors with whom she had worked. "Oh, can I," she replied, "but not on your ninny will I."

Watching Miss D. over the years, I became convinced that acting has to be inside you, a calling, an appetite. So few people ever see beyond the surface of it, beyond the so-called glitter. When we were on location, I got up at 4:30 or 5:00 in the morning, and Miss D. half an hour later. We ate our eggs— now not hard-boiled—in silence. She was preparing herself to do her job and it was no time for fun and jokes. That attitude carries over onto the set.

I am always amused when others are surprised that Miss D. doesn't live or think like a stereotypical "Hollywood movie queen"—whatever that is. When Miss D. goes anywhere, if only to the market, she makes a point of looking the way a film star is expected to look, which means dressing well, wearing makeup, hair well-groomed. She was dressed that way the first time we met, when she interviewed me. She never refuses an autograph, and when she gets a request for a photograph she signs it herself. Her fans sense in her a caring person. Many fan letters ask for her advice in the most intimate areas: whether they should marry, divorce, change jobs, and, in one instance, whether a daughter should expose the fact that her stepfather had sexually abused her. In this case, Miss D. did not feel qualified to give advice.

She became my role model, whether by design or accident or just closeness I can't say. She showed great patience with me in those beginning months. I had a troubling habit of saying "okay," one of those annoying things that makes you wonder why you spent a fortune on a college education. Once, when I was on the telephone, she told me she had counted fifteen "okays." She decided that every time I said "okay" I would owe her a quarter. In two weeks I had broken the habit, or I would have been broke.

41

In the 1970s, Miss D. made a record album in England, *Miss Bette Davis Sings* produced by Norman Newell for EMI. It was released in the United States some time later. Among the songs she sang were, "They're Either Too Young or Too Old," "I've Written a Letter to Daddy" (from her film *What Ever Happened to Baby Jane?*), "Until It's Time for You to Go," and one of her very favorite songs, "I Wish You Love."

Miss D. accepted an invitation to autograph her album at Tower Records in Los Angeles, one day from three to six in the afternoon. Both of us thought she would sign a few albums and that would be that. When we arrived at the record store, the line of people stretched completely around the block, and some of them claimed they had spent the night so they would be sure to get in. Miss D. stayed and signed autographs until the store ran out of records and, finally, way after dark, we went home. Young people, old people, even actor friends came for an autographed album. For weeks afterward she received albums in the mail, to be signed for people who had been turned away.

It has been written often enough that Miss D. intimidates people—reporters frequently; other actors and actresses on occasion. I can only say that they have never seen the fun and humor in her that I have seen. She is not one to let a holiday slip by uncelebrated. She creates a backdrop suitable for each occasion. On Washington's Birthday she serves cherry pie to go with dinner—and once she dressed like Martha Washington. On St. Patrick's Day we dressed like leprechauns. One Christmas we were living in a hotel, and I went shopping and we had all the decorations and frills of home.

One Easter I bought her a baby rabbit and left him in her room while she slept. Of course, the rabbit immediately ran under her bed and I had to shoo him out. I waited for her to wake and let out a bloodcurdling yell. At first she didn't even see him. Then she sat up in bed and said, very calmly, "What's that over in the corner?" The rabbit wouldn't move. He was so still he didn't look real. Then he moved and, back in the bed, all one could see were those Bette Davis Eyes.

She adored the rabbit, whom we named Mr. Brier, but the amount of traveling we did forced us to give him away.

There have been no dull moments in my years with Miss D., and I can say with certainty that in a crisis she is at her calmest. It is little things that test her patience. But when friends think, "Oh God, what a blow, let's not tell her"—nonsense, she can handle those moments. She may wish the problem wasn't there, but she can always rise to the occasion.

Such a time came, in triplicate, during the long summer of 1983. It was in June that she underwent her mastectomy, followed nine days later by a stroke, and still later that year by a broken hip. She has given me great credit for helping her in the hospital, but to the extent that I did, it was only because of what she had taught me. I was a mild, almost docile person when I came to her. Had her illnesses occurred earlier in our relationship, I doubt that I would have been strong enough or tough enough to fight for her, when necessary, against the wishes of her nurses and sometimes her doctors. This book grew out of that ordeal. One of my own lasting memories is of waiting for her to come out of surgery. Knowing how close we were, the doctors had broken the rule and allowed me in the operating room, dressed in a surgical gown. Through a large wall-to-wall window I could see the doctors in the next operating room peering into Miss Davis's room. It could have been a scene from a movie.

When the surgery was completed, the nurses kept insisting that I wait in the lobby or go to our room. They kept saying that she was under such heavy medication that she would never know whether I was there or not. I refused to go. I said, "Look, she may be sedated, but she *knows* what is going on. I will wait. She'll know I'm here and if she needs something I'll be near."

I meant those words, but the argument was soon academic. Within minutes after they wheeled Miss D. out of surgery, she was awake and talking. None of her doctors could remember having a patient given so much anesthetic who could revive so quickly and be talking. As Miss D. was wheeled by, she gave me a wink, and ten minutes later she was talking to me. She was overcome with thanks when she realized that I had put in her hand her tiny lucky china sleeping cat, which B.D. had given her years before, and without which she would not go anywhere, especially on a plane. She named the cat Nerack.

After the stroke I stayed in her room night and day for eight weeks, not knowing if or when she would be out of danger, and waiting for any signs to tell us the Bette Davis we all knew would be herself again. The signs began to come two weeks later. She was definitely on the mend. When the doctors told us she would probably never work again, her lawyer and great friend Harold Schiff corrected them: "Yes, she will. You just don't know Bette Davis."

Someone else who stood by both of us was my beau. Miss D. encouraged me to call him in Paris whenever I felt the need. The sound of his voice always helped give me the strength I had to have.

So now we have come to the closing of my chapter. When I came to work for Miss D. I had a feeling—and I have never been very intuitive—that the job would last five or six years. We went a little beyond that, and a long way beyond the definition of a job. She is the most honest person I ever met, a friend and mentor, and more. I know she hates to make a mistake, but how quick she is to admit when she has made one. I know what she has tried to give back to her profession, quietly and privately. The seminars she has attended and the talks she has given to aspiring young actors. She has never hesitated to help a student who she thinks has talent.

Miss D.'s great understanding of youth and parents today has helped me relate better to my own mother and father, and vice versa. I remember one day telling Miss D. that I didn't think

44

my parents understood me or the path I've chosen to take in my life. She said, "Kath, you must march to the beat of your own drum, but maybe when you see your parents you have a chip on your shoulder and don't give them a chance to understand you. It's a very common situation in families after the children start maturing." My first instinct was to quickly deny this, but knowing Miss D., I was sure there was truth in what she said. I hated to admit it. I was judging my parents and trying to change them as well. I think it's a very common mistake made by both parents and children. I followed Miss D.'s suggestion when I next saw my parents, and what a difference it made. She made me realize what it must be like being a parent. Miss D. would tell me, when I had my own children to remember it's not what you say, it's what you do. I saw her practice what she preached with her children.

I have written her replies to so many fan letters—into the thousands—all those years that I feel I should not leave without adding one of my own:

My Dear Miss D., Mother M.:

On Friday, June 13, 1979, we met; a little girl from San Bernardino not really knowing who Bette Davis was, or anything about her profession. You taught me so many things:

To have great care in doing whatever it is one does; to fight for what you believe is right and to admit when you are wrong; to be a part of life and not watch it go by; to accept the risk of failing, and the risk of feeling; to know love and recognize hate; to understand that if everyone likes you, there must be something wrong.

You said you had a hunch about me, one for which I am forever grateful. I will cherish all our experiences, from our first trip to London to the last, and the delight of working with you on these pages.

You will be with me wherever I am. On another trip to Paris, you teased me and gave me a new nickname. I will sign off with it now. If the meaning of it is unclear to anyone else, no matter. You know and you're the one who counts.

Always my love,
Gigi

FOUR

WELL ON OUR WAY

AMONG MY POSSESSIONS is an embroidered pillow that says, "Old Age Ain't No Place for Sissies." I had found out this was the understatement of all time. When Kathryn and I opened the door to our house in Los Angeles after an absence of nearly five months, we were beside ourselves with joy to be back among familiar things. It was fun seeing once more the many photographs with famous people on my walls. I have two favorites, one with Anwar el-Sadat and one with Mae West. Mae, Beverly Sills and I were photographed together at a dinner given in our honor by my friend Chuck Pollack. I had always wanted to meet Mae West and so had Beverly Sills. Not long afterward Miss West invited Chuck and me to her apartment for drinks. It was fascinating. Everything was pure white, with lots of satin materials. We were completely impressed with her butler-houseman, who all through our visit stayed in the next room—out of sight but on hand immediately if Miss

49

West said a word to him. It was a legend in Hollywood that Mae West's bedroom had a ceiling of mirrors over her bed. I really wanted to check it out. I thought I would go to the powder room and "sneak a peek," but I lost my nerve. The agility of her manservant scared me. If I had been caught of course he'd tell her. I certainly didn't want that to happen. Her shoes did have twelve-inch heels. She did not talk the way she did when she said, "Beulah, peel me a grape." She asked me immediately if I had a lover. "Not for very many years, Miss West," I answered. She advised me to do something about this. I have consistently ignored her advice in this matter.

When we were leaving my home in Hollywood to fly to New York for my mastectomy, I stood in the doorway for a long time and said, "I wonder when I'll be home again," then slowly closed the door.

Our return home had pitfalls we had no way of anticipating. I was not the same person who had left in June, nor was Kathryn. At home the changes became apparent.

It has been said that life is what happens to you while you are planning something else. At that point my plan was to get completely well. On our arrival home, we realized we needed a cook. For the last twenty years I had done my own cooking, but very soon I knew I was no longer able to do so. We started a search which turned into a "cook's tour." One after another came to be interviewed. In and out, for a total count of thirty-five. They were of diverse sizes and ages and backgrounds, but all had one thing in common, they couldn't cook. Not one of them could fry an egg or mash a potato. Some of them packed and snuck out in the middle of the night. One was doubled up in pain on her first day. She told us she was having menstrual cramps. We sent her home in a taxi and told her to come back the next day. She did, worked for a few hours, and, not saying a word, walked.

Kathryn was looking forward to the arrival of her beau from

France. It was an exciting time for her and helped her forget the travails of finding a cook. Prior to my illness we had decided it was time for Kathryn to live somewhere on her own. She would still do the fan mail and other necessary secretarial duties, but she would no longer live with me. I fully agreed that at her age it was time for her to have her own home. She had gotten me through the worst of my medical problems and home again, and she was still reminding me, "We'll make it." We had so far.

A friend suggested that Kathryn should have a checkup. She came home with devastating news. The doctor had found a growth under her left arm which might or might not be malignant. He told her she might have lymphatic cancer, with six months to live if not treated properly, and there was the possibility of a double mastectomy. I can barely scratch the surface of what we both felt. She had suffered through my surgery and the aftermath, and now both of us faced the possibility that she might have the same dread disease. We had no answers, only questions.

Should she tell her beau before he came? Would he "walk"? What would happen to her hopes, her plans for the visit and indeed her future? It was a frightening experience, and one Kathryn, after all she had been through with me, did not deserve.

The day Kathryn went to the hospital to have the lump removed, I waited at home in torment. That afternoon she called to tell me that the surgeon who was to operate on her told her the lump had disappeared. Whatever the reason, Kathryn and I had been through a needless fright. We were both beside ourselves with joy. Now she could welcome her beau from France with an unclouded mind.

We were not through with misfortunes yet. One day I fell and broke my hip. The next day Kathryn and I found ourselves in an ambulance going to another hospital for another operation. This was certainly the straw that broke the camel's back—as well as my hip. It was not the most severe kind of break, so I was allowed to go home a few days after the operation. Quite naturally, I was unable to walk. After the stroke my walk was completely normal, and this setback to my recovery was crushing. I had to learn to walk all over again.

For the next three weeks, Kath was vacationing with her beau, and I was at home with my parade of cooks. Peggy Shannon, who had been my hairdresser and my friend for many years, came to see me as often as she could. Gertrude, a nurse, turned out to be a lifesaver while Kathryn was away, not as a nurse but as a friend.

I said no to friends when they wanted to visit me. I did not want anybody to see my home with these strange characters trooping through it. I survived those three weeks with hardly a decent meal or anyone to help. I kept a brown paper bag in the wastebasket next to my bed. I ate all my meals in my bedroom during this time, so I could pitch the inedible food into it and not be rude to the cooks. This problem, though it had overtones of comedy, was not good for my health. All my film career I had envied Katharine Hepburn's high cheekbones and narrow face. Now I had them.

Kathryn eventually lived in San Francisco. For the next few months she flew in on weekends as often as possible to see me, which definitely saved my sanity. In addition to dozens of cooks, Kathryn also interviewed replacements for her job. One candidate, after having three days off, returned with three young men to stand by while she packed and "negotiated" her salary. Even though we negotiated, she still walked. Another young girl had come for the day and Kathryn showed her what her duties would be. She started at 10:00 A.M., and had a two-hour lunch break. When we called her to ask her to come back the next day she refused, saying the day before had exhausted her. She was obviously unable to replace Kathryn. Our search for a replacement led to an interview with a very elegantly dressed woman. Impressed that she wasn't in dungarees, I hired her instantly. I had trouble with her last name. Instead of saying "Fireshaker," I would sometimes say "Cracker," which embarrassed me very much. This elegant, proper, secretarial type spent one whole night packing secretly in her room and snuck off early in the morning, borrowing my car. She had clearly made arrangements to cash her two-week check, even though she had worked only a few days. It should be noted she returned the car, but as it turned out, she was a cracker.

Kathryn and I often felt that we were writing a script authored by Erma Bombeck. As far as the cooks who came in and out, my biggest distress was the hundreds of dollars' worth of food that was wasted. The cooks bought for their own taste and even hid the food. I would find well-known store-bought cookies that they claimed, when they served them, to have baked themselves—these were often hidden behind the dish towels in a drawer. One cook even went so far as to serve me Stouffer's bell peppers with a tomato sauce, which I instantly recognized. She had cooked the Stouffer's peppers, claiming they were hers. To assure myself I was right, I looked in the rubbish and found the Stouffer's box. Needless to say, another one bit the dust.

I was at my wit's end, growing more depressed daily by the time Kathryn flew in from San Francisco for one of her visits. She immediately realized I had about given up, and she would not allow this to happen after all we had been through. That afternoon she made reservations at the San Ysidro Ranch, a famous vacation spot in Santa Barbara, for the weekend. She knew I desperately needed to get back into the world. I had been so preoccupied with my everyday survival and so caught up in my own misery that I almost rejected the hand Kathryn held out to me. It was one of those on-and-off, up-and-down tugs-of-war. I wanted to go but kept saying no. When Kathryn threatened to leave and never come back, I finished dressing and followed her out the door, grumbling as I got into the car, doing my best to be disagreeable. Once or twice she broke the silence between my outbursts to say, "We'll make it." At that moment, I don't think either one of us believed it.

By hook or crook we finally did arrive at the San Ysidro Ranch. This trip was the first time I had been outside my own home since my arrival home for Thanksgiving. That night, to be in a beautiful dining room with other people was a wonderment to me after all this time. The wonderment, however, didn't prevent me from continuing to tell Kathryn how miserable I was. My behavior was enough to ruin my career, as my whispers can be heard around the world. That Kathryn took it and kept her temper should have earned her the Croix de Guerre. The next day we drove into Santa Barbara to look around. I had recovered my disposition, allowing myself to fully enjoy lunch and dinner in the dining room, plus a before-dinner visit to the bar, where a pianist played all the old tunes. I sang along with him.

After my return from this fun weekend I no longer wanted to stay cooped up day after day. Eventually Kathryn moved back to LA and had her own home. She felt that renting a house at the beach would be the best thing for my complete recovery. She decided that she would find an apartment nearby whatever house she found for me—a mind-boggling, practically impossible assignment; but find them she did. As her apartment was unfurnished, she asked me to go shopping with her to buy furniture. We went from Marina Del Rey all around LA, even into Burbank. From 9:00 A.M. to 6:00 P.M., we went to small stores and large stores, involving miles of walking. This was the next step in my complete recovery.

One day while shopping we went to a restaurant for lunch. Everyone seemed to recognize me and many asked for my autograph. Much to my amazement I was thrilled. I said to Kathryn, "I can't believe it. I have missed being famous and made a fuss over." I had missed it. Talk about coming in from the cold!

Kathryn found a house for me practically in the ocean, with a lovely patio that had the look of a rain forest: many huge cacti, elephant ears, palm trees, banana trees and geraniums, all on a hillside going up from the patio to the road above. The house was in Malibu, a famous seaside town for actors. All sand and surf, rocks and canyons. Living by the ocean again, where I had lived so often in former years, and which I adored, turned out to be exactly what I needed for my complete recovery.

In spite of the rapture of living by the sea, we had not put behind us the worst of our cook problems. Again they came in and out. Four in the first month including one who claimed that her mother had held *my* mother, when a baby, in her arms, in Tewksbury, Massachusetts. Not only couldn't she cook, but she claimed she would make me well. If she had stayed it would have been the opposite—no doubt I would have had another stroke. Another one bit the dust.

I moved into my house in the middle of July, a little over a year after my surgery and stroke. Kathryn had been right to recommend the move to the beach. For the first time since my return home, I started to entertain old friends—R.J. Wagner, Roddy McDowall, Jill St. John, Marion Rosenberg and the great hairdresser Jose Eber. I was nervous about having my friends see me. Would they think I looked different? I gave a dinner party in Malibu for them. I told them how frightened I had been that they would think I looked different. R.J. laughed and said he was petrified to come, thinking that I *would* look different.

It was a warm and affectionate night. One and all were overjoyed that there was no sign of what I had been through. Another hurdle—seeing old friends—was behind me. There was a swimming pool at Kathryn's apartment. One day with great trepidation I decided to try it. Could I still swim? I found I was able to, in spite of my broken hip and my weak left arm. There were tears in Kathryn's and my eyes, and hugs and kisses, and of course Kathryn saying, "Miss D., we made it!"

FIVE

LOVERS
AND
OTHER STRANGERS

As I grow older, when looking back, I realize I was always in love with "being in love," seldom really in love. This was an important condition for me to be in. The world looked brighter, I felt I looked prettier, my performances were definitely better. Hedda Hopper, the famous columnist, once remarked about this in her column: "Bette Davis' best performances are when she is in love." How right Miss Hopper was.

Dark Victory, George Brent. *All About Eve*, Gary Merrill, whom I later married. My first real love was my first husband, Ham Nelson. There is no doubt about it, a girl's first exposure to sex is a powerful drug. Even after we were divorced, I still loved him and saw him often. In truth, I am always self-conscious that I, as a Yankee-bred girl, have been married four times. If I had been brought up differently, morally speaking, I probably would have had affairs with the men I married and maybe never have married any of them. I thoroughly approve of living with a man you love before marriage.

At a party in Hollywood one night, the conversation turned to unfavorable remarks about women who had been married many times. Obviously, all concerned forgot I had been married many times. As the talk continued, I thought about my four husbands and, without realizing it, jumped to my feet and said, "One died!" I have always believed that being married was the ideal way for a woman to live.

When I was sixteen I slapped my date when he said something I didn't like. He didn't hit me back, as I guess he should have. He said, "This is something a girl should never do." I never did again.

When I was nineteen, I was proposed to by a student at Yale with the proviso that I give up my desire to have a career as an actress. He put a ring on my finger. I wore it for four or five days, then returned it, telling him it would be impossible for me to comply with his request. Thank God even at that age I was wise enough to do what I did. Had I agreed to give up my desire for an acting career, all through the years I would have wondered if I could have been a success as an actress.

In the twenty-odd years since my divorce from Gary Merrill, I have not married. I have been tempted twice; therefore I am able to provide two ways to lose at love.

One of my prospective husbands was a Catholic, with a very possessive mother. He was a splendidly obedient son, almost to the point of slavery. She was horrified at the prospect of our marriage, on the grounds that (1) she might lose him; (2) I was older; and (3) I was not a Catholic.

The only problem I could do something about was Number 3, so I decided to become a Catholic. The first step was to make an appointment for an interview with a priest, who came to my suite at the Plaza Hotel in New York. Two hours and five or six scotches later, he was still sitting on my couch, enraptured at being in the same room with Bette Davis.

I helped steady him as he weaved his way out of my room. That was the end of my attempt to become a Catholic. The obedient son's mother saw to the rest.

At the time of my second serious involvement, I promised my lawyer that I would not marry again without a marital contract. It should be clear by now that in matters of the heart, I was in need of guidance. If I am representative of those who share my astrological sign, Aries women are the most romantic fools that ever walked the earth.

I was in England making a movie. My fiancé flew there to be with me. One evening over cocktails, I took a deep breath and said, "There are papers you have to sign before our marriage."

He looked at me blankly and said, "What do you mean?"

I said, "You must sign a premarital agreement. These papers will confirm what's mine is mine and so forth."

The next morning I went off to the studio. When I returned to the hotel that evening, I asked at the desk if he was in his room. The clerk told me he had checked out earlier in the day.

It was a terrible blow to my pride. I was understandably heartbroken. That was the last time I have given marriage any serious thought. Fortunately, I usually bounce back quickly from any heartbreak. There was always the work I adored which always stood by me.

I was almost sixty when I met and fell in love with a very young man—young enough that I never considered marrying him. I enjoyed so much being with him. We had such fun together.

Over one New Year's holiday, we rented a house at Lake Arrowhead with a group of friends that included my sister, Bobby. One day we went antiquing, exploring the little shops that I have been drawn to all my life, with their charm and occasional hidden treasures. I bought a bureau I have always loved having in my house. The shopkeeper was thrilled at my being in her shop. She said, "Would you and your son care for a drink?" Never have I been so embarrassed.

61

I've usually fallen in love with men younger than I—older men are usually so settled in their ways. Our society does not yet accept the older woman who marries a younger man. Of course it is permissible for men to marry younger women. No one thinks much about it. But an older woman with a younger man is laughed at behind her back. It is one of our more curious taboos, when you consider that women stay sexually young much longer than men.

In the mid-1970s, when I was doing my one-woman show in London, a lady in the audience at the Palladium asked me, "How do you know who likes you for yourself or for who you are?"

Terrific question. I sometimes don't know. I've never worried about it. I would rather have a go at something I feel, and be hurt, than always be protecting myself—that way one does not really live.

With age I have become a bit wiser about the climbers and users. B.D. had a fine sense of spotting them, the young men who were attracted to her because they wanted to meet her mother, or to say they had dated the daughter of Bette Davis.

I have often advised young women to beware of a man who never cries, or a man who uses tears to get what he wants. I have known men who consider it a test of manhood to show no more feeling than a Greek statue. Look for the man who falls somewhere in the middle.

I would also advise any woman against having an affair with a married man believing he will ever leave his wife, no matter how often he says his wife does not understand him. Love is not as necessary to a man's happiness as it is to a woman's. If her marriage is satisfactory, a woman will seldom stray. A man can be totally contented and still be out howling at the moon.

Divorce is failure. But it is better to fail than to continue in an unhappy marriage. On two points, I make no apology. I never left my husband for another man, and to me no divorce is ever a friendly divorce. If you are still friendly then for heaven's sake stay married and work it out. I am bored to death with divorced couples who claim they still love each other.

Among the reasons marriages fail, sex ranks no higher than fourth, behind money, having only one bathroom, and an inability to communicate, reasons one, two and three.

Many years ago I recorded a song called "Single." It was written as an answer to Richard Burton's successful record about marriage being the ideal state. I think the words to "Single" are more applicable to the feelings of women today, old and young. Moreover, I think men are responsible in great part for women feeling this way about marriage. Many women would rather be single for all the reasons given in the lyrics of the song:

Single,
It's so nice to be single
To be comfortably all alone
So nice to own
A small apartment's only set of keys
To lock the door and shut off the phone
And lie around and do whatever you please.

Single
It's so good to be single
It's so good not to listen to
Some idiot who's convinced
He's heaven's gift to womankind
Who criticizes whatever you do
And spouts about a man's superior mind.

If I want to eat candy
I want to eat candy
And not be reminded about
The inches on somewhere or other.

63

BETTE DAVIS

If I want to be lazy
I want to be lazy
Without being lectured about
That monster he has for a mother.

Married
I will never get married
And I treasure my civil rights
To stand and fight
Against the tide that roars
Be somebody's wife
Convention
Get me out of my sight
I'm much too much in love
With a single life.

Find myself a husband
Did you say "husband"?
He hates you if you wear
Kid curlers in your hair
And facial cream
Will make him meet his maker
But acid fairly drips
From his sweet-as-honey lips
If you wake up not resembling
Caroll Baker

Spend hours on his meals
Spaghetti sauce and veal
But he says, "don't serve me that
*   TV dinner"*
You end up eating pills
And fighting over bills
Till you're prematurely gray
And he's Yul Brynner.

I'm so glad that I'm
Single
I'd much rather be
Single

Just imagine how nice to be
Alone with me
To take my bath
And sing off-key
With none to nag
Or disagree
If I take pickles with my tea
To watch TV or turn it off
Blow my nose or sneeze or cough
And not be told I've caught a cold
Or even worse.

I'm getting old
Keep your married life
I'd rather be
Free . . . free . . . free
I'd rather be
Single.

Two people deeply in love feel they will be able to adjust their differences after they are married. To accomplish this one or the other has to give in. Too often in America the husband is the one who gives in. Let's say a woman is tired of staying at home and wants to go out at night. When her husband comes home a wreck from his work, she expects him to take her out. If he asserts himself and refuses because he is too tired, I feel that his wife should respect his decision. Also, she should not continue to try to rule the roost.

I contend that working women make better wives. They understand how much hard work goes into making a dollar. For this reason they are more considerate about squandering their husband's money and they understand how weary he may be at the end of the day.

My daughter was brought up by a working mother. Because of this she was a knowledgeable wife. I would come home from the studio when B.D. was growing up, and from the minute I came through the door, no one spoke. B.D. had a drink prepared for me. I would sit down, finish the drink, and that would relax me just enough to be ready for a conversation. Women who have never worked do not know about this need for "recovery" time.

There are male subjects and female subjects for conversation. Men are just not interested in hearing how the washing machine broke down or what little Johnny did all day. Spare me any cries or laments about my viewpoints being dated or submissive. Marriage by its nature is less fair to women. Adam didn't cook and he never spent enough time with Cain and Abel.

Of the men I didn't marry, the dearest was George Brent. I fell in love with George years before we ever became an item. He helped me through some difficult personal problems during the making of *Dark Victory* and also fell in love with me. I often hoped he would want to marry me. He never did. In 1975, I saw George in San Diego when I was on tour with The Bette Davis Show. I had not seen him for nearly twenty years. He sent me a bouquet of orchids backstage with a note asking if he could see me before the show, so he could "duck out" afterward before he was recognized. I had half my makeup on when the orchids arrived. In spite of myself, I felt a rush of excitement. I said to my hairdresser, "Let's make me look as good as possible before George arrives. I want him to see me looking the best I can after all these years." The George Brent of my past, of so many movies and so many memories, walked into my dressing room. He had changed a lot. Why not? So had I. I might have felt sad and a little cheated except for one rather nice reminder. As he left, George giggled. He still had that same crazy, infectious giggle I remembered so well.

Almost as many inhumanities are committed in the name of love as in the name of religion. Love is always trouble. What can you do about it? There are only two things—either stop loving or give a lot more love. Then you will be in more trouble. Then give a lot *more* love.

I have always declined to play the pointless game of separating sex and love, trying to explain the difference, measuring one without the other or the damage done to a caring heart when either is missing. If you do not know where the line is drawn, you're on your own.

I mean it when I say that "sex is God's joke on human beings." This quote has been translated into multiple languages and rebroadcast to the armed forces overseas. And I haven't changed my opinion. Sometimes when I watch television a face will appear out of the mist of bygone years, someone I once knew better than others. It always brings back special memories.

Most women have a special sexual fantasy. Mine was to make love on a bed covered with gardenias. Once I was involved with a man famous in the music world, a composer and orchestra leader. He was, I suppose, what I had once hoped Ham Nelson would be. We were both married, not very happily, and my marriage was soon to end. His went on. He was one of those who would not leave his wife. I did not expect him to do otherwise.

As we were both famous, our affair had to be a discreet one. Discretion is tiring, often nerve-wracking, and therefore such affairs usually are of limited duration. He wrote a song for me.

One day at the height of our romance, he reserved a suite at the Waldorf-Astoria in New York. To my delight and amazement, the bed was covered with gardenias. When the maids were tidying up the room next day, what did they think of a wastebasket filled with very wilted gardenias?

Long after the affair had run its course, I was in a nightclub where his orchestra was playing. He danced with me and told me that he had written the song the orchestra was playing about our romance. To this day, whenever I hear that song or see a gardenia I think of him.

On my seventy-fifth birthday, I came home after a working

day. When I walked into my *salle de bain*, to my utter amazement there was champagne, caviar and a bathtub full of floating gardenias. I counted them. There were seventy-five. There was a note inside one of the champagne glasses saying, "Happy Birthday. See you shortly."

I promised myself years ago that when I was old and gray and looked back on my life, I would have no regrets in the romance area. I have kept that promise. When I fell in love and felt romantically inclined I did not ignore my desires.

There is a song, "Someone to Watch over Me." This, I felt, was the perfect kind of man for me to marry. I never found him. I imagine no man ever felt this way about me, because I was and still am capable of managing my own life and could not imagine I would like to be "watched over." I'm still hoping one day I'll find him. I am the eternal optimist, always have been.

One of my most amusing crushes was inhibited by the fact that the object of my affections, who invited me quite often to his house for dinner et cetera, each time displayed with pride garden vegetables and homemade butter sent to him from the farm of his former mistress. Since I had no farm I could hardly compete.

Another object of my affections (and he felt the same way) turned out to be a Communist with a party card. He tried to make me a party member, but he did not succeed. With his gorgeous car and all his money, I found his political beliefs ridiculous. We had a date for a rendezvous in Mexico. To my chagrin I waited and waited. He never came. He had stood me up. In this case I had not followed my own advice. He was married.

As I am writing this, it seems I was often a loser in the love game. A most popular bachelor at the time in Hollywood had a yen for me. While he was with a naval unit during the war, in New Jersey, he told me to keep "looking up," because one day he would fly a blimp over my house in New Hampshire. I, of course, took this with a grain of salt. I was wrong. One day, lo and behold, a blimp flew over my house. It caused a sensation in the little town of Franconia, where I lived. I imagined the local citizens suspected that it had some connection with me. It was a topic of conversation for many days. I have to admit, I was pretty impressed by this prank. I was only more impressed with attention from the sky by Howard Hughes, who used to buzz my house in Manhattan Beach on his way to Russia or Afghanistan or you name it.

There is a poem by Carl Sandburg that I adapted for my show *The World of Carl Sandburg,* calling it "Meditations on the Forms of Love." It seems to be an appropriate ending for this chapter:

Love; is it a cat with claws and wild mate screams in the black night?

Love. L-O-V-E, is it a tug at the heart that comes high and costs, always costs, as long as you have it?

Love, is it a free glad spender, ready to spend to the limit and then go head over heels in debt?

Love, can it hit one without hitting two, and leave the one lost and groping?

Love: I said Love, love can you pick it up like a mouse and put it in your pocket and take it to your room and bring it out of your pocket and say, "Oh, here is my love, my little pretty mousey love"?

Yes, love, this little word you hear about; is love an elephant and you step out of the way when the elephant comes trampling, tromping, traveling with big feet and long flaps of drooping ears and ivory tusks, and you step out of the way with respect . . .

Is love an elephant? Or a snake, say like a rattlesnake, like a creeping, winding, slithering rattlesnake with fangs, poison fangs they tell me, and when the bite of it gets you, then you run crying for help if you don't fall cold and dead on the way—

Can love be a snake? Or would you say love is like a

flamingo with pink feathers, a soft sunset pink, a sweet gleaming naked pink . . .

Or could it be, love is a big red apple and you don't know whether to bite into it . . . I'm asking, kind sir, is love a big red apple?

Maybe it's goofer dust . . . and when your man sleeps you sprinkle it in his shoes and he's helpless and from then on he can't get away from you, for he's snared and tangled and can't keep from loving you—could goofer dust be the answer?

And are they after beguiling and befoozling us when they tell us love is a rose, a red, red rose . . . just one more flame of a rose that came with its red blush and crimson bloom and did the best it could with what it had and nobody wins, nobody loses, and what's one more rose? . . .

I had the good fortune to perform this glorious poem every night on the tour of the Carl Sandburg show. I've lived through most of these varied loves. Most certainly Goofer Dust. And especially the love that is a red, red rose. And nobody wins and nobody loses.

SIX

THE SEVENTIES

MY CAREER NOT ONLY SURVIVED in the 1970s, but grew because of television. I spent most of my creative hours in this medium, except for the many months I toured with The Bette Davis Show in England, Australia and the United States.

I was a frequent guest on the most popular television talk shows of the decade—those hosted by Johnny Carson, Mike Douglas, Merv Griffin, Dick Cavett. One of those appearances became historic among those who saw and heard it. Dick Cavett asked me when I stopped being a virgin. With my eyes popping out of my head, and counting to ten, I said, "When I married my first husband." Then, after a long silence, I said, "And it was *hell* waiting."

On another Cavett show I was asked by Tommy Smothers, of the brother comedy team, "Miss Davis, would you let me mess around with you a little?" After I recovered from the shock, I joined the audience in several minutes of helpless laughter. Upon reflection, I could not help being flattered that a young man would want to "mess around" with someone so much older.

In other ways television had given me a friendly reception. I was being offered Movie of the Week scripts, plus many specials; the scripts were equal to what was being shown in motion picture theaters, where the "real films" were on display. I resent the snobbery that makes a distinction between the so-called "real films" and the films made for television. It is the same snobbery New York theater people once felt about motion picture actors. The television films are just as well done.

All this nostalgia about the "golden age" of Hollywood is almost laughable. Hollywood hasn't changed in the ways that count. No matter how we romanticize them, the golden years were hard work, as they are today. The fight is still between the artists and the money men.

For an actor, the Old Hollywood had one distinct advantage: the contract system, as much as we may have felt abused by it. With the contract system you made one picture right after another. It might take ten years, but with a little luck along the way you could become a star. You had to contend with a good share of inferior scripts in the beginning, but in spite of this the public gradually got to know you.

There is no continuity to careers anymore. They no longer write scripts for actors, they just *cast* them. We used to become a part of the audience's lives. There was a vast machinery behind us, huge publicity departments. Reading a newspaper today you will see huge ads for films you never heard of, starring young players you have heard of even less.

In the final analysis, a good picture cannot be harmed, nor a poor one helped, by the size of the screen. In 1973, I costarred with Ray Milland in an NBC Movie of the Week called *Scream, Pretty Peggy*. The film had a Peggy in it, but no screams—except for my silent ones.

I have never hesitated to admit when a film I made was junk. And I reserve the right to be proud of the ones I knew to be good. A few years ago, a reporter asked me how I liked making all those soap operas "years ago." The question puzzled me. "What soap operas?" I said. "Well, you know," she said, *"Now, Voyager, Dark Victory, Payment on Demand, The Great Lie."* I think I showed my restraint by not pulling her hair out by the roots. If those were soap operas, give me more.

During those television years I did them all: *General Electric Theater, Alfred Hitchcock Presents, Perry Mason.* I sang and danced on *The Andy Williams Show.* I also guest-starred on *Laugh-In*, a zany comedy-variety show and clearly a departure for me. There was one other role reversal: I interviewed Mrs. Rosalynn Carter when she was First Lady. I appeared with Jimmy Durante and Milton Berle on their shows. And I went Western, as a guest star on *Gunsmoke, The Virginian* and *Wagon Train.* All of these Westerns were filmed without a dressing room on the set, which I had been used to. Instead, one sat between shots for hours amidst dust, grime and (no delicate way to say this) horse droppings. You not only acted the part of a pioneer woman, you felt like one.

I had decided, long before most of my contemporaries, that television was going to be a lasting and powerful presence in our lives. It was the New Medium. During those years scripts for "real films" were hard to come by in Hollywood. You had to accept a different set of rules for television. You had to realize it was not like Warner Bros., all those years before. You had to shut up and not complain. When word got "around" that I was accepting the new order, I had more offers than time to read them.

A famous blonde sex symbol never learned that lesson. Offered a series, she demanded all the old Metro courtesies, including a car and chauffeur waiting at the stage door. She didn't know we had to be good sports and forget the past luxuries provided for us as stars.

An exception was Robert Wagner, who had known the glory and the customs of Old Hollywood. He had been a part of it. When I appeared in his series, *It Takes a Thief*, for the first time in my television career I had a dressing room with MISS BETTE DAVIS on the door and flowers on my makeup table. I had not enjoyed such treatment since I had left Warners. It was nice to have a mirror and lights and a heated room when you arrived at the studio, with the sun just rising.

A year later, I worked with Robert on a television movie called *Madame Sin*. It was filmed in England. The picture was to be released in Europe, but had been planned as a pilot for a network series. This was one of five or six pilots I made during these years, none of which ever sold.

I remember this film for reasons unrelated to its success or failure. It is the custom in many present-day films, whether for television or theaters, for each actor to wear a hidden body microphone. This technique became essential with the loss of soundstages and today's trend toward using natural sets—the real houses and the "real" everything. The sound man is unable to get the big boom mikes near enough to us to hear what we are saying. The more intimate devices do eliminate much of the dubbing afterward, a long, tedious process.

On the set of *Madame Sin* one day, I felt a tug and blurted out, "My microphone has slipped." Robert, partly to be funny and partly out of reflex, put his hand under my skirt, trying to find the microphone and put it back in place. I do not recall how high I jumped, but the reaction on the set was hilarious. I call Robert beautiful and that he is—inside and out.

None of us are fans of these body mikes, which are miserable to wear and tend not to stay in place, whether they are clipped to your bra or skirt or tucked into the fold of your collar. It is a little like being wired as an undercover cop, I imagine.

When R.J. asked me to make a trailer (a short film used to advertise a coming film) for *Madame Sin*, I was less than thrilled but suspected nothing. I told him I had never believed in trailers for my films but would do one for him. A makeup man was on hand and Edith Head was in the studio to see that my wardrobe was correct. That most talented of Hollywood designers, Edith often said and has been widely quoted, "No one drops a mink like Bette Davis."

A camera crew stood by. All of it was a setup. In walked Ralph Edwards, creator of the successful television show *This Is Your Life*. The format of this show took you through your entire life. Those who appeared on the show with you were all surprise guests, invited to talk about you when they knew you. R.J. and Edith were coconspirators. I could have killed them both. Friends of mine had been hidden all over town so I would never know who was to appear.

Olivia De Havilland was flown in from France. Willie Wyler was there. Benny Baker, a comedian who had given me my first screen kiss. After the show was over I felt as if I had been to my own funeral.

During the seventies, I lost my beloved sister, Bobby. I will always miss her. Also, my son, Michael, became a husband. My older daughter, B.D., gave me a second grandson, named Justin. I entered my seventieth year, made the swing from the big screen to the smaller one, and received awards in such numbers as to test one's credulity. And shelf space.

In a long career, you sometimes find yourself competing with your own past. In *The Disappearance of Aimee*, I played the mother of Aimee Semple McPherson. I had all but begged to play the part of the evangelist twenty-five years earlier. In this made-for-television movie, she was played by Faye Dunaway.

I can imagine no circumstances under which I would work again with Miss Dunaway. It is possible she feels the same about me, but I believe I have the stronger claim. We filmed *The Disappearance of Aimee* in Denver, in the summer, and day after day Miss Dunaway kept the cast and crew waiting. She had a fondness for riding around town all night in a chauffeur-driven limousine, sipping champagne in the backseat. I did not mind her nocturnal habits so much as I did the daily delays while she had her makeup fixed, ad infinitum.

The summer heat was stifling. One day she held up the schedule for hours, while nearly two thousand extras sweltered in a church that could not be air-conditioned. As a rule, these are the best of fans—unpaid, there for a box lunch and a glimpse of the stars. They ought not to be treated with discourtesy. To help pass the time, I went onstage and sang "I've Written a Letter to Daddy" from *Baby Jane*.

The film was difficult for me in another sense. I was disappointed by Miss Dunaway's portrayal of Aimee Semple McPherson. I had seen the evangelist once at the Foursquare Gospel church, had heard her on radio many times, and had begged for years to be allowed to play her. At the time no studio would touch the story; the censors would never permit a film about a woman who was the head of a church and was also a whore. So I ended up later playing her mother.

I was busy through most of the decade, shooting other films such as a four-hour version of Thomas Tryon's *The Dark Secret of Harvest Home*, *White Mama* and *Strangers: The Story of a Mother and Daughter*. For this performance I won my second Emmy.

I was thrilled to be given a part in *Death on the Nile*. It provided me with the chance to work with David Niven and Peter Ustinov. I had great respect for the talents of both of them and had even more than the usual difficulty in getting any sleep the night before a first day of shooting.

That day I had trouble with my lines; something that seldom happened to me. Later, chatting after work, I confided that the thought of working with the two of them had scared me sleepless. They exchanged glances. Niven laughed and said, "Then we're even. Neither of us slept a wink either, we were so petrified to work with you."

Niven and Ustinov were part of a superb cast that included Angela Lansbury and Maggie Smith. I had reservations that went beyond the script and the actors. When my agent, Robert Lantz, first told me I had been offered a part in this film based on an Agatha Christie book and it would be filmed in Egypt, I said to him: "But what if they start a war while I'm there?"

Robbie replied, "They wouldn't dare."

This was one of those occasions when the making of the movie was a story in itself. To begin with, I was starting *Harvest Home* at the time I agreed to appear in *Death on the Nile*. For this reason, I was given a stop date for *Harvest Home*—a point at which I had to be released from the schedule, a concession companies rarely give. For that concession I could credit the fondness felt for me by Lew Wasserman, the head of the studio, who had been my agent for many years.

The film dragged on and it was clear to me that we could not meet the stop date. The set was disorganized. A brilliant cameraman was fired. I asked Robbie Lantz to discuss the problem with Wasserman, who responded by saying how much he loved me. We did get Lew's assurance that my scenes would not be cut to meet the schedule. Instead, I worked Sundays and late at night in order to reach Egypt nearly on time.

With my hairdresser, Peggy Shannon, I left the *Harvest Home* location in Mentor, Ohio, stopped off at my home in Connecticut to repack, and arrived in Cairo four days later. From there we flew to Aswan, where *Death on the Nile* was filming. It is safe to say we were reasonably travel-weary when we arrived. At the hotel, I was greeted by the director, John Guillermin, with the words: "Well, I see you finally got here." And a little later: "See that you know your lines."

There was no remark more likely to offend me professionally. I *always* knew my lines. At our first meeting, in Robbie Lantz's office, I had found no humor in Mr. Guillermin. But I did come to respect him greatly as a director.

To reach the *Carnock*, the tiny old boat where the filming took place, a speedboat carried the cast back and forth up the Nile. A speedboat was a first for me and I was terrified. Then came the final day of shooting on location in Egypt. We all wore old-fashioned clothes and shoes and were supposed to walk to shore across a gangplank the width of one board. I took it upon myself to tell Mr. Guillermin, "It would be impossible to walk on that plank. I would never make it. I'll fall in."

It was ridiculous to ask any of us to risk it in those period costumes (which, by the way, were brilliant and won an Oscar for Anthony Powell). Shortly a great many Egyptians were summoned to build us a proper walk. While the work went on, I watched from the rail of the *Carnock*, wondering if we would make our flight to London that evening. From the deck below, Mr. Guillermin called up to me, "Miss Davis, we are building the Santa Monica Thruway for you."

The cast was grateful to me. If it seems that others waited for me to speak out—I usually do.

That remarkable cast also included Olivia Hussey, who had come to prominence as Juliet, in the picture directed by Zeffirelli. She played all sorts of East Indian chants on a stereo in her dressing room. It drove me mad. I politely asked her if, at six o'clock in the morning, she would not play those records? She did not speak to me again on the *Carnock* or acknowledge my presence for the rest of the shooting.

I especially enjoyed working with Maggie Smith, who played the companion to my rich dowager. Maggie and I felt a few more scenes between us would have been an addition to the film. The relationship between our characters was hilarious.

A few years later, I was substituting for Dinah Shore at a function in Washington. A chair from the set of the show *All in the Family* was to be presented to the Smithsonian Institution, and in Dinah's place I was the hostess. Anwar el-Sadat was at the White House that day, with President Carter and Israel's

Mother, look at our socks!

One of very few "cheesecake" photos of me taken back then.

My big thrill—meeting W. Somerset Maugham on the set of *The Little Foxes*. The amused listener in the middle is Harry Crocker, a member of the Hollywood press.

The Petrified Forest, my second film with Leslie Howard, made Bogart a star.

Ruthie meeting me in New York upon my return from London in 1940.
A future president—who could have known then? *(Photo courtesy of Lester Glassner)*

Photographed during the filming of *The Great Lie*. My romance with George Brent ended up a great lie.

Working as a hostess at the Hollywood Canteen.

In the Eddie Cantor film *Thank
Your Lucky Stars*, I told my
partner to forget I was Bette Davis.
He did. I felt like the woman
on the flying trapeze.

In *Now, Voyager* Paul Henreid lit two cigarettes at a time and it became a legend, copied all over the world.

Claude Rains and me in *Mrs. Skeffington*. He was my favorite and most admired actor. It was a great help in playing Fanny Skeffington to have my wardrobe done by Orry-Kelly and my hairdo by Maggie Donovan.

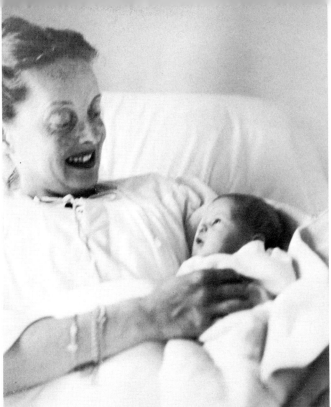

One-day-old B.D.
in the arms of the
happiest woman in
the world.

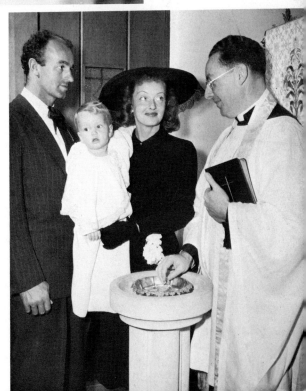

B.D.'s christening—a
prophecy of things to come.

At Laguna Beach with B.D., my sister Bobby, and her daughter, Faye—all in mother-daughter dresses in honor of Thanksgiving.

No need to identify this film. *All About Eve*, with two recognizable faces, Anne Baxter and George Sanders, was the movie debut of Marilyn Monroe.

At the party after filming *Payment on Demand*, holding a present from the crew telling me I was a "good egg."

Gary's and my present to B.D., a sister we named Margot.

Of all sad words of tongue or pen, the saddest are "It might have been."

On the beach in front of our house in Maine, with my three smashing children, Michael, B.D., and Margot.

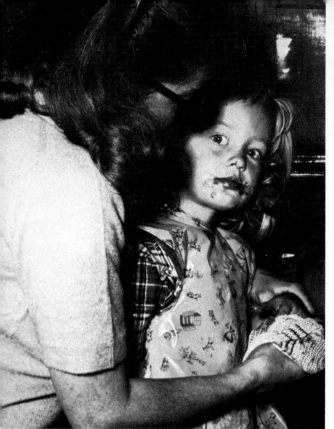

B.D.'s start at becoming a great cook. I think she ate more than she cooked.

B.D. on her tenth birthday holding my present to her—a blue-point Siamese cat.

A favorite photo of
Michael and me. We all
agreed that he was an
adorable little boy.

Darling Michael during his years
at the Fessenden School in
Massachusetts. His beloved dog
was always waiting for his
holiday homecoming.

The B.D.s on board the SS *Independence*, destination Gibraltar. From there we went to Madrid, where I played Catherine the Great in the film *John Paul Jones*, starring Robert Stack.

With B.D., my favorite traveling companion, in front of St. Peter's in Rome, holding up objects to be blessed by the pope, who appeared daily in a window high above the square in front of St. Peter's.

Menachem Begin, planning the agenda that would lead to the historic Camp David meetings.

A security man mentioned to Sadat that I was in a room across the hall from where the three leaders were debating matters that had to do with the rearrangement of the universe. I was standing in the doorway a half hour later when Sadat emerged, crossed the hall, hugged and kissed me.

He was very dark, not tall, a man who seemed coiled with energy and warmth toward his fellow man. I saw him then as one of the great hopes of this century, a Harry Truman figure, born a peasant, later a revolutionary and a prisoner of war, then a loyal public servant who for two decades had been in the shadow of the more flamboyant Gamal Nasser. When Sadat was murdered in 1981, I was reminded once again how very hard it is to replace those whose courage and ideals the world depends on.

In 1977, my mind was much closer to home. Whatever price I had paid during my career, all seemed worthwhile when I became the fifth person, and the first woman, to receive the Life Achievement Award from the American Film Institute. My predecessors were John Ford, James Cagney, Orson Welles and William Wyler.

Jane Fonda was smashing as the mistress of ceremonies. Her father was one of the speakers. At my table were Robert Wagner, Olivia De Havilland and Joseph Mankiewicz, who directed *All About Eve*.

But for me the high point, one that captured the decade and possibly my career, came when Willie Wyler spoke. He recalled the only professional fight we ever had, when I disagreed with him over the ending of *The Letter*. I walked off the set in anger, but of course returned a few minutes later—and played the scene Wyler's way.

Willie's speech was short and funny and had the added advantage of being true. He said, "If tonight I brought up the subject of the last scene in *The Letter*, Bette would insist on going back to Warner Brothers and reshooting it the way she wanted it." Over thirty years had passed. This brought down the house.

It was an extraordinary night, as I made clear in my own remarks: "To me this is the frosting on the cake of my career. I am truly overcome. In 1926, from Lowell, Massachusetts, came Ruth Elizabeth Davis, known as Bette, who was not beautiful, not tall and willowy, who had a tiny voice that couldn't be heard past the first row of the theater. She didn't know whether she had talent, but she did have drive and ambition. . . ."

Those qualities I have never lost. And age, I believe I can truthfully say, has not done much to bank whatever fires burned inside me.

On my seventieth birthday, to observe the occasion properly, I gave a party, hung a black wreath on the front door, wore a black dress, put on blackface, and wore a black Afro wig. Being seventy made me feel as if I should be in mourning.

And, as they sometimes did, my words came back to haunt or at least amuse me. I had, on a much earlier birthday, described the ages of woman: "Don't let anyone ever kid you that life begins at forty. At forty, I thought that was really the end. Then came fifty—and my children didn't help any by making it even more of a monumental moment with their references to half a century. 'Mother Half-a-Century.' Ideally, women should stop growing physically older at forty and men at fifty. What a wonderful world that would be." So I said. So I felt. I will now trouble that thought no further.

In the late 1970s, I considered it an honor to be asked to appear on *60 Minutes*, and to be interviewed by Mike Wallace. My children would be part of the program. B.D.'s interview was to be videotaped at her farm in Pennsylvania; my son, Michael, at his law office in Boston. Mr. Wallace tried very hard in these two sessions to worm out of B.D. and Mike an admission that, as a famous woman, I was less than the ideal mother. He did not win with either one. I was so proud watching the show. These excerpts will show I had a reason to be proud. First, B.D.:

Q: I gather you enjoy being the daughter of Bette Davis?

B.D.: I enjoy being my mother's daughter. As a person. But I don't, I've never really related to being the daughter of a famous person, per se. It has always been there. It has never bothered me particularly.

Q: Well, how come it has not bothered you and yet it does bother so many children of so many important people?

B.D.: The only thing I can attribute it to is just what we talked about. She was always very, very, very concerned with Hollywood being a place, not a way of life. And she worked very hard at that. She worked very hard to have a home in Maine, which was way out in the country on the seacoast. And my brother and I had farm animals. There was nobody to take care of those farm animals but us. And if we hadn't taken care of them they would have disappeared. And . . . she was very concerned with teaching us responsibility. The values of the real world, as well as enjoying the fun of Hollywood life. She didn't take that away from us. But she made us realize there was a difference. And I think the contrast made both my brother and I aware of the world as it was, and able to take what we wanted from it.

Q: Was she a tough mother?

B.D.: In certain ways.

Q: What ways?

B.D.: Discipline, manners. It was worth your life to forget a "please" or a "thank you." And things that I consider important in raising my children, really. As far as fun things went, she was totally lenient.

Q: Like . . .

B.D.: Oh, we never had curfews. I was allowed to date who I pleased. She totally trusted my judgment as to who my friends were. Where I went, and with whom, because she felt that at a certain age—a fact that I agree with—your children have gleaned all they can from their parents. And they have to start fending for themselves. It doesn't mean you're not there to help, to protect, to listen. But basically you can no longer steer. You have to step back and guide. And I think she realized that. And at a very young age she stepped back and said, all right, you're a thinking person, go think.

Q: And as far as you know, she had no objection to the fact that you got married at the age of sixteen? On the contrary, she gave it her blessing?

B.D.: Yes. I don't think she expected it to work out. She expected me home again. As a matter of fact, around our seventh anniversary she announced that she had given up, that I wasn't coming home. That I was fairly well stuck where I was . . . but then she believed in allowing me to make my own judgments, my own mistakes.

Q: You're making this sound like a storybook. . . .

B.D.: No, no. We had arguments. We certainly did.

Q: Who doesn't? But no, no real disadvantages to having been the daughter of Bette Davis?

B.D.: None. None that I found.

Q: Is she vain?

B.D.: I would say no. There's a story, and she tells it on herself, that she was going to have her eyes or her face fixed, lifted. And she had the appointment all made and the time came and she . . . backed out. And she's always made a big point out of being straightforward about her age. And that, well, that goes back to her New England ethic. Honesty, I think, is probably the most important single thing in Mother's life.

Q: That can get a little tough for the object of the honesty, though.

B.D.: Oh, she's painfully honest about everything.

Q: And humorless, one hears.

B.D.: It's difficult for Mother to laugh at things. She takes everything seriously. Most of our differences, arguments, whatever you want to term them, have been over the fact that I am devoted to finding everything funny. And that bothers her. I mean, when I have something serious happen to me, there's always a funny side. Always. And that upsets her, because she doesn't think that I take life the way it should be taken, which is deadly serious.

Q: Joan Crawford's daughter, Christina, wrote in her book . . . you know what's coming . . .

B.D.: I know about the book. I don't exactly know what question is coming.

Q: Well, she wrote that during her growing-up years she came to depend rather heavily on the servants for a sense of continuity, because her mother wasn't around a lot of the time. Her nurse . . . became the central person in her life. Now, Bette Davis was a huge and busy star . . . did she have time for you?

B.D.: Yes. She made time. Part of the reason was that she had me travel with her almost everywhere, all the time. And I guess part of the reason also was that, when she was home, she was home. She wasn't too busy. She was to be with her children to do things with us.

Q: Was she a star at home?

B.D.: No, never, never. She was in blue jeans and work shirts and she was a working mother when she was at home. She was in her kitchen. She was tidying up the house. She was weeding her garden and planting bulbs. She was a mother.

How proud I was that B.D. seemed so completely approving of me as a parent. My greatest compliment as a mother was the day she told me she was bringing up her sons the way she and Michael were brought up.

Michael's interview followed B.D.'s:

Q: Your sister says she doesn't have much of a sense of humor.

MICHAEL: My sister says that about my mother? I don't know what she means by that in terms of—

Q: Life is real, life is earnest, and there aren't many jokes around Bette Davis.

MICHAEL: I don't believe that's true at all. To say that she is humorless, or whatever the word was, is wrong in my opinion. I've joked with mother quite often and she and I have a marvelous rapport when we get together. . . .

Q: What kind of a mother-in-law is she?

MICHAEL: You have to ask my wife.

Q: Maybe I will. What do *you* think?

MICHAEL: Well, I think she has been fantastic with us. She doesn't impose at all. She will ask if we want to come visit with her and if we do, we do. If we don't she says, fine, there will be a better time. You know, we do like to stay close. And I don't think she puts any demands on Chou-Chou as a mother-in-law, in any ways.

Q: From talking to you and your sister . . . I get the impression that she's really a pretty good mother. I mean, a woman you admire and adore.

MICHAEL: Right. There's no doubt. Because when you think how she brought us up and the circumstances she was in, having her career, having trouble with her husband, and having to move us back and forth across the country, and being that star that she is, it's tremendous when you think about what she has done. . . .

While watching the show, I was amused by the debate between B.D. and Michael over whether or not I had a sense of humor. I, of course, was on Michael's side.

Soon after the show aired on CBS, I was to leave for England to film *Watcher in the Woods*, which was Kathryn's first film with me. In New York, she had learned to cue me. At one point, she looked up and asked if I were paid by the page. I laughed and said, "If I'm paid by the page I will be broke by the end of this one."

The part was a short one. I worked only some ten days in the six weeks we were there, and actually had time to prune the geraniums daily in the garden of the Berystede Inn, where we stayed. The days were not uneventful. One morning at six, as we came out of the hotel to leave for work, there was a flash of light. We had been caught by a photographer, whom we felt sure came from one of the London papers. We were right. Next day, on the front page of the *Daily Express*, was the photograph, plus a headline which read: "Bette Davis Doesn't Give a Damn How She Looks." I was incensed. What would I wear going to work at six in the morning? A gold-lamé evening gown?

This started a correspondence between the *Daily Express* and me. The *Express* printed the contents of my first letter, omitting the part that made them look like idiots. This provoked me into writing another letter even more insulting, and they did not print it for obvious reasons. However, the paper gave one of its columnists instructions to write a glowing article about me. That was worth a good laugh to Kath and me.

While in England, I learned that I had been nominated for an Emmy for Best Actress for my role in *Strangers*. The teleplay had been two years in the writing. The producers had approached me that far in advance, outlined the story and asked if I would be interested in playing the mother. I was.

In the story, a daughter tries to regain the love of her mother after a separation of twenty years. Finally the daughter reveals that she is dying of cancer. Gena Rowlands played the daughter brilliantly. I had casting approval. The script was filled with speeches that amounted to full-page monologues. I wanted badly to win that Emmy. I felt I deserved it, if not for the performance I gave, then for the difficulty of the part and the hardships of the filming. The setting was a Rhode Island summer, but we worked in the bitter winter cold of Montecito, in northern California.

I had asked B.D. to phone me in London if the news was good the night of the Emmy Awards. Mine was the last given, the very last after a two-and-a-half-hour show. I had by then lost all hope that I had won. Around four in the morning, the phone rang. I picked up the receiver to be greeted with B.D.'s joyful shout: "You won!"

The producers were understanding enough to excuse me from the set the next day. I was a wreck from anxiety and no sleep. That evening Kathryn planned a special dinner in my honor, served in our suite, which we called "The Watch Tower." We had a strategic view in this lovely English inn, the kind for which the word *quaint* seemed to have been invented. A popular place for local weddings.

In our suite there was an alcove in the shape of a tower, and out of its window we could observe all that went on. Daily attractions consisted mostly of weddings, which provided a range of entertainment: seeing if we approved of the bride, the dresses of the bridesmaids, and if we agreed that the groom was good-looking. We also had fun watching the people who came for the traditional English high teas. Often, to our annoyance, at the oddest hours we were required to participate in fire drills.

One drill started in the middle of the night, in the rain. I tossed a coat over my nightgown and climbed out a window facing the roof. We felt this was safer than using the stairs. I called back to Kathryn: "The cigarettes. My God, don't forget the cigarettes." Before we left England, we gave a fireman's hat to each member of the staff as a memento of our stay. When we checked out, they were all standing in line, wearing their hats.

After *Watcher*, I started a more challenging film called *White Mama*, a title the network kept insisting had to be changed. I sent back word that I would refuse to make the picture if they changed the title. They didn't.

White Mama was an agonizing picture to make: the story of a white woman and the abandoned black ghetto youth she befriends, played superbly by Ernest Harden, Jr. We filmed it on location in East Los Angeles, in the Skid Row area, where one must walk around drunks passed out in doorways. Once I had a bottle thrown at me. Under these conditions, the film was directed with a sensitive touch by Jackie Cooper, the onetime child actor.

Over the years, my life has been a series of wars, one crisis after another after another. But there was also fun and pleasure along the way. In 1979 I was the guest of honor at one of the Dean Martin roasts. The speakers were Henry Fonda, Vincent Price and Howard Cosell.

Hank Fonda said, "I've been close to Bette Davis for thirty-eight years, and I have the cigarette burns to prove it." And a gag telegram was read from the American Tobacco Institute—at least, I think it was a gag—thanking me for my contribution to that industry. "'No one,'" Dean Martin read from the telegram, "'swings her butt the way Bette Davis does.'"

Perhaps this is the place to explain how and why I became famous for smoking. I was, when I arrived in Hollywood, a very prim and proper Yankee girl. Wore no makeup, except for a touch of lipstick, and no sexy clothes. Was obviously an innocent in the whole area of sex. I didn't seem to measure up in my own mind to the image of a typical actress. So to offset this weakness socially, I learned to smoke, which made me feel very sophisticated.

Later I discovered that for a performance a cigarette is a marvelous prop—sometimes for emphasis, sometimes for anger. For so many things. What emotions you can convey merely by putting one out. If I played a character who smoked, I didn't just take a puff or two in one scene only. I smoked all through the film, as any serious smoker would.

SEVEN

THE BETTE DAVIS SHOW: IN PERSON AND ON FILM

E N ROUTE TO AUSTRALIA to do The Bette Davis Show, as the lights of Sydney, Australia, twinkled below us, the captain spoke over the intercom, inviting me to come forward to the cockpit. I was to be treated to a spectacular view of the city at night as we landed.

I went through the door to the cockpit and heard a roar of laughter. Quite by accident, at that moment the Fasten Seat Belt sign was put on.

I realized I had been paid a great compliment. A planeload of international passengers had remembered a line from one of my films, *All About Eve*.

Bette Davis in Person and on Film was just that: one hour of scenes from films and one hour, sometimes more, of questions from the audience. The first tour was in 1973, repeated off and on during the following years and as late as 1978. We were usually in a different city each night. The tours included twenty-six states in the U.S., two weeks in Australia and six months in England, thousands of fans wherever we went, and theaters new, old, grand, small, elegant and decrepit.

After the film was finished, I would walk onstage smoking a cigarette, slowly look around, cross to a table, put out my cigarette, look once more at the audience, and say, "What a dump." With that familiar, drawn-out phrase the ice was broken. It told the people in the audience they could sit back, relax and laugh; I was not there to be worshiped.

This theatrical format challenged me. The questions were varied. Some were very personal and many had to do with my career. It was rewarding to discover that my audience did not consist mainly of blue-haired ladies on a nostalgia trip. Many were young people, college students, some of them not even born when I won my second Oscar, in 1938, for *Jezebel*.

I cannot explain why so many come whenever or wherever I appear. But then, I could not explain a career that has lasted over fifty years, or my "place" (as it is called) in the industry, or why an audience will cheer and applaud on hearing certain lines from *All About Eve*, or *Cabin in the Cotton*, or *Beyond the Forest*. Maybe they are all part of the same answer.

Easier to deal with was a question a lady asked me in Perth, Australia. "Miss Davis," she said, "why do people have such strong emotions about you? My husband wouldn't come with me tonight because he hates you."

I said, "My dear, one can never be a success in my profession if everyone likes you. When you get home tell your husband he is one of many who feel the same way about me."

These performances grew out of an idea developed by John Springer, a veteran Broadway press agent. Springer produced a series of one-woman shows under the title Legendary Ladies of the Movies. I was invited to be the first. On February 11, 1973, the series opened at Town Hall on West Forty-third Street in New York City.

I wore a gown of black velvet trimmed in white satin. After

the film scenes were over, the lights came up and I walked onstage. I was given a standing ovation.

All day I had been fidgety and nervous, with good reason. I didn't know if this format would work and please an audience that paid for its tickets, if there would be a full house, or how I would be received. My doubts were unfounded. Every seat was sold.

In 1974 my tour ended in Hartford, Connecticut. The night before, I had celebrated my sixty-sixth birthday on the stage of Symphony Hall in Boston. The whole evening was a "love-in" for a hometown girl. How could I have known when, as a child, I often went to Symphony Hall that one day I would be on the stage of this famous building?

My son was in the audience that night. It was the first time he realized how famous his mother was, as the crowd cheered, applauded, and rose as one.

The traveling each day was grueling and the schedule frantic. In May 1978 we toured southern California. In Pasadena, the question-and-answer period was a free-for-all, and this excerpt is fairly typical of the exchange across the footlights:

Q: *(From a man)* What will you be doing after the show?

A: I'm going home to bed—alone.

Q: Thank you for bringing countless moments of pleasure to me, my mother, my grandmother . . . oh, am I making you sound old?

A: I *am* old. My seventieth birthday was a few weeks ago. *(Huge applause)* I'm glad you think it's something to clap about.

Q: Is there a star you most wanted to work with and never did?

A: Charles Laughton. I wanted a script for us to make about the two meanest people in the world.

Q: What leading man impressed you most?

A: I assume you mean professionally? I worked with so many greats. But most impressive was Claude Rains.

95

Q: Did you have a feud with Errol Flynn?

A: In his autobiography he says I clawed his face in *Elizabeth and Essex* with one of my royal rings. It's a lie. Anything cruel I do is mental, not physical.

Q: Why are there so few good contemporary films?

A: There have never been many good films in any year. Five or sometimes ten.

Q: Would you like to see a movie based on your own life?

A: No. I am against biographical films made while the person is still living.

Q: Who would play you?

A: Someone peculiar.

At the London Palladium, a woman asked, "Miss Davis, have you ever had your face lifted?" I asked her to come down to the stage. In the far recesses of the theater, a lady started walking down the aisle. It was a long walk and she looked petrified. I guess she thought I might hit her. When she arrived, I walked to the edge of the stage, knelt down with my face out over the footlights so she could see me clearly, and said, "Don't you think I'd look better if I *had* had a facelift?"

Where these answers came from, night after night, out of what well or spring, I never really knew. Peggy Shannon, my traveling companion, was with me every mile of the way and knew how unrehearsed my responses were.

London was the scene of a great triumph. I had been booked for a tour of England by the impresario Billy Marsh, with one night only at the Palladium in London. The night I arrived, Mr. Marsh came to my suite at the Grosvenor House Hotel. He told me that a week before, he had placed a small announcement in the London *Times* that I would appear at the Palladium on a certain date. Before the day was over, a line a block long appeared outside the box office. The one night became four nights at the Palladium. Every performance was packed.

My personal life was relatively stable in those years, meaning that I had avoided getting married again. But the campaign for better scripts and better directors still had to be waged. The fight was endless and would never really be won, only renewed. I missed the battles of another era. The Bette Davis Show kept me busy through part of the decade. The tours were valuable because they showed me that movie fans, far from being the fickle creatures we often paint them to be, are capable of incredible loyalty.

I have in mind another memory of that night at the Symphony Hall in Boston. As I was being asked questions from the audience, a voice in the balcony called out, "Do you want an ice cream soda?" How I realized who it was, I'll never know. Of course, the Maine accent was a help. I then answered back from the stage, "Are you Francis Young, from Southwest Harbor, Maine?"

I then told the audience who he was: the first boy I ever kissed. To say that this embarrassed Francis Young, standing there in the audience, is the understatement of the year, I'm sure.

When I was a young girl, every day I walked to the pharmacy, not necessarily for an ice cream soda. Every day, he would come to where I was sitting and ask if I wanted an ice cream soda. I would order one and just look across the counter at his beautiful brown eyes. He walked me home one day and kissed me. All this took place in Southwest Harbor, Maine, where Mother had rented a house for the summer.

Then the summer ended and we went away. More than fifty years later, in Boston, I heard his voice again. I invited him to come backstage after the show. I should have realized that after fifty years he could hardly still have those beautiful brown eyes. In this respect, I may be fortunate. Friends are not surprised when they see me years later. They have kept up with me as I have grown older on the screen.

I agree with Thomas Wolfe—you can't go home again. This can also apply to people's memories. And that was my regret in seeing Francis Young. In doing so, I lost the memory of the first boy I ever kissed, in particular, his beautiful brown eyes.

I always closed my show with a favorite line from *Cabin in the Cotton*, one of my first films at Warner Bros. Richard Barthelmess was the star. "I'd luv to kiss ya, but I just washed my hair" was the line. The most thrilling evenings of the show were the four nights at the Palladium in London and three nights at the fabulous opera house in Sydney, Australia. It was hard to say, "What a dump!" in both of those places. They are fabulous!

EIGHT

THE EIGHTIES

I T IS SAID THAT WE KNOW we are growing older when police officers and bankers and judges start looking as though they had just graduated from high school.

So it was that I reacted less than gleefully after I signed to star in *Skyward* in 1980, and learned my director would be a young man named Ron Howard. I asked fellow actors if they had heard of him. Most of them had. "Oh, yes," they said, "he's in *Happy Days* and long before that he was the little boy, Opie, on the old *Andy Griffith Show*."

Apparently he heard I had reservations about him, because he called me in New York. I told him I usually have choice of directors. He kept assuring me, "Everything will be all right, Miss Davis." I said, "Well, we shall see."

We filmed *Skyward* in Dallas, Texas. The first day on the set Mr. Howard went assuredly ahead directing me, which was exactly the right way to handle my disapproval. It would have been fatal to show any fear of me. He then would have cooked his goose (especially in the unbelievable heat in Dallas). As he said on the telephone in New York, "Everything will be all right." It was evident on the first day that everything would be all right.

The film was a pleasant one to make except for the intolerable heat and electrical storms. The temperature in Dallas that summer reached the 100-degree mark at seven in the morning and at two o'clock it was always 130 degrees.

One day the heat from the asphalt at the airport, where we were shooting, melted the soles of my sneakers. The crew covered the asphalt with boards, which was a help. My character was a pilot, so it was necessary to wear a flight suit and sit for hours in the cockpit of a mock airplane. At one point I told Ron Howard and our producer, Anson Williams, I did not think I could survive on the set another day.

Eighty people died of the heat in Dallas that week. I was truly fearful the same thing might happen to me. I told them I would not work the next day if the temperature did not change. The temperature didn't change. Still, as you've guessed, I went to work, thinking, the show must go on, and that kind of idiotic professionalism.

Skyward was about a fourteen-year-old girl, a paraplegic, who dreams of escaping from her wheelchair and, by learning to fly, she does. A real paraplegic, Suzy Gilstrap, played the part. I totally disapproved of this kind of realism. I thought the film would be better served by giving this opportunity, a super acting part, to an actress who could act as if she were paralyzed. I also felt it was cruel, if not exploitative, to expose Suzy to a new world which, from a talent standpoint, it was obvious she could never be a part of. My director and producer totally disagreed with me. They were enraptured at the idea of casting a person who was actually handicapped as the paraplegic.

The morale on the set was high. I always try to give some type of token present to each person who participates in making a film. Kath and I decided to give each and everyone T-shirts with letters on the back saying, "Bye you-awl. Bette D." Unbeknownst to me, the cast and crew had all pitched in and bought me a little gold airplane to add to my charm bracelet. Among my most treasured possessions are the presents from crews on a film. I consider such gifts to be a supreme compliment to the actor who is the recipient.

In the winter and early spring of 1981, this time in snow and below-zero temperatures on Long Island, I made a television film called *Family Reunion*. It was the story of a widely scattered New England family whose less noble members were engaged in a land heist. I played a retired schoolteacher who convenes all the relatives to prevent this skullduggery from happening.

After reading the script, I said to Lucy Jarvis, the producer, "There is a part for an eleven-year-old boy, right?"

"Yes, there is," said Lucy, "do you have someone in mind?"

"Yes, I have. My eleven-year-old grandson, Ashley Hyman."

Ashley was the son of my daughter, B.D. B.D. and I often commented that Ashley might have talent as an actor. After returning from whatever motion picture he had seen, he would impersonate some actor in the film. In particular, I remember how he reenacted all the scenes from *The Pink Panther* over and over. He was utterly delighted with himself. He had reason to be. He was good.

Miss Jarvis interviewed Ashley and was willing to go along with my judgment and gamble on him. And oh, what a gamble it was. I knew if he couldn't make it, I would have to find a replacement for him. I also knew that would most certainly break his heart and affect his future, since he would feel he had failed in something he was excited about doing.

The day we rehearsed our first scene I had no idea what to expect. He was terrific. He hit his marks, remembered his lines, did all the right things. From then on, I was not frightened for him. B.D. and I were right.

Ashley is very bright. And so he became totally fascinated with all the technical things related to filmmaking. He wanted to see what the cameraman was doing, what the sound man was doing, what everyone was doing. His curiosity was understandable.

The only advice I ever gave him during the making of the film was: *"Concentrate."* That meant to think only about his performance. Do not be distracted by anything else. That is a great necessity for any actor: to keep your mind on your performance.

I thought his ability to adapt was impressive. He had left home, was away from his parents, really, for the first time in his life. He was living in a country club on Long Island, keeping up his schooling with fifteen hours of tutoring each week, and reporting not long after dawn each day to a motion picture set—something he had never before even seen.

I should not have been surprised at his poise. Ashley was really super in school plays from the time he was in kindergarten. He has been an actor virtually from birth. I have seen him give a performance at home that would win awards (as his mother did before him . . . and his grandmother). I found out that he had a great deal more of B.D. in him than I realized. Down the line we are all very dramatic, great exaggerators. We never talk in hundreds, we talk in millions.

B.D. is the biggest exaggerator of us all, from the time she was a little girl. As she grew older her reminiscences of her younger years made very good stories, but had very little to do with the actual happenings. I must admit they were always amusing.

Kathryn was in complete charge of Ashley during the filming. She, Peggy Shannon and I dubbed ourselves "The Three Witches." Kathryn saw to it that Ashley learned his lines and was responsible for him on and off the set. Ashley adored having Kathryn in charge, as she was a very bright, pretty young girl, and from the day Ashley was born he loved pretty girls. I see no reason for him to change as he grows older.

Kathryn also kept Ashley busy when he was not filming. In addition to keeping up with his schoolwork, they went roller-skating, took long walks, jogged most days, took squash lessons at the club, and spent long hours planning surprises for me.

Kath and Ashley, who insisted on having helium balloons for my birthday party, searched Long Island for them for days. He found games to be played in my room during the cocktail hour, and he ordered delicious hors d'oeuvres and spent hours making decorations, including the biggest surprise of all: a five-foot wall-to-wall poster made of glitter and ornaments he had collected during his strolls with Kathryn.

I was so touched that an eleven-year-old boy would go to so much trouble for his grandmother. The quality of the dinner he ordered, and the imagination he showed about the decorations, were due to knowledge of these things he had learned from his mother.

At times Ashley was ornery, like any eleven-year-old boy, but basically his behavior was remarkable. He loved the life at the Piping Rock Country Club, the commotion of the picture set, just all of it!

During the filming of *Family Reunion*, Kath and I noticed that when he was any distance away from the director, Ashley did not hear his instructions. It seemed to everyone he was not paying attention, an unforgivable thing to do to a director. When it happened several times, we wondered whether there was something wrong with his hearing. Also, when Kath asked Ashley to do something, she was annoyed that he seemed to be paying no attention to her. We called Ashley's mother to get permission to take him to a hearing specialist. She said, "Forget it. We've been told about this by many of his teachers and we've just dismissed it. If you want to waste your money, go ahead."

We went ahead. The director, Fielder Cook, gave Kath permission to make appointments with a doctor, even if it was inconvenient for him to plan filming without Ashley. We were given the name of one of the top hearing specialists in the country, who practiced on Long Island.

We found out an amazing thing. Ashley's hearing was impaired a great deal because of an eraser lodged in his nasal passage, probably as a result of his putting that end of a pencil up his nose, absentmindedly, as a little boy. The eraser was removed and the examination continued. Finding this eraser did away with the many headaches he had had for years. No more aspirin daily.

He was then put in a soundproof room with a microphone. The examination continued for a couple of hours, with many machines monitoring him. He was examined from different angles, sometimes behind, sometimes way across the room. The reports came back from the lab saying he was forty percent deaf in his left ear.

The doctor felt sure that to a certain extent Ashley had learned to lip read. He recommended a small hearing aid that Ashley could wear on the bow of his eyeglasses, which, fortunately, Ashley had worn for a long time. The first evening he wore the glasses with the hearing aid attached, everytime I spoke he said, "Grammas [his name for me], don't talk so loud." We laughed. He was jumping up and down with joy, hearing so many sounds he had never heard before.

I worried that wearing a hearing aid would embarrass him and make him insecure when among people. I was relieved that it did not faze him. He was so overjoyed to be able to hear. So were we. We played the record "Celebration" over and over that evening.

Ashley had never seen his grandmother work. I had a long scene, a long speech in a high school auditorium. Ashley was sitting out in front with the other students. I caught a glimpse of him out of the corner of my eye. He was so visibly impressed, so proud, that it was a warm and poignant moment for his grandmother.

People will argue that talent, a certain kind of talent, skips a generation. So do certain diseases. His family and I know that it is up to Ashley to decide whether he goes on with acting, or if *Family Reunion* was a one-time experience. I asked him the day before he left what he had learned from making the film. He answered, "How hard you have worked all your life, Grammas."

If he learned that acting is a hard job, he absorbed an important lesson, should he choose it as a career.

An unusual footnote about the film was the fact that nine children of well-known actors were in the cast. The list included Roberta Wallach, daughter of Eli Wallach and Anne Jackson; Christopher Murray, son of Hope Lange and Don Murray; Rikke Borge, daughter of Victor Borge (and granddaughter of composer Richard Rodgers); and Julie Garfield, daughter of the late John Garfield. John Shea, who did not have famous parents, played the part of my nephew in the film. He gave a super performance. I feel he will eventually have an important career.

A year later, Ashley and I were given awards for our performances in *Family Reunion* by the Film Advisory Board. The presentation ceremony was in the ballroom of the Hilton Hotel in Beverly Hills. Ashley flew to California for the event. As we stood in the receiving line, he whispered, "What do I do, Grammas?"

"You just smile. Smile at everybody."

"But I don't know anybody," he said.

"Doesn't matter. Smile anyway."

It turned out to be a most glamorous affair—including a torchlight parade by the waiters, and many presents for Ashley and me. The gorgeous flower arrangements were donated by a florist named Arturo, because of his longtime admiration of my work. He has continued to shower me with floral presents ever since.

Shortly after *Family Reunion*, I gave a housewarming party, the first one since my latest move to California. Among my many guests were Edith Head and Natalie Wood. As I said good night to them both, how could I possibly know that was the last time I would ever see them? I was asked to give the eulogy at Edith Head's funeral. In the church, Elizabeth Taylor and I were in the same pew. It was a wry coincidence, as Miss Taylor was in Los Angeles performing in the stage version of *The Little Foxes*, one of my old films.

Having never given a eulogy before, I was nervous. The church was filled to the brim with people who respected and loved Edith. Hollywood will never have another clothes designer to equal her. She dressed me for *All About Eve*, *Madame Sin*, *June Bride* and *A Pocketful of Miracles*.

My favorite director, William Wyler, also died in this decade. The same was true of him as it was of Edith. There will never be another as talented in every area of filmmaking as Willie: scripts, performances, editing, everything. His films will be an inspiration, I feel, to many future directors. As I used to say while being directed by him in *Jezebel*, *The Letter*, *The Little Foxes*, if Willie told me to jump in the Hudson River, I would. That is how much faith I had in his opinion of my performances.

So many greats have gone in the seventies and eighties. How I miss them all. There seems to be no one to replace them.

As I grew older, starting with being seventy in particular, I decided to lessen the shock of hearing the actual age by adding the numbers together. At seventy-four I was eleven. I first disclosed this idea in an interview with David Hartman on *Good Morning America*, and I have given it to many of my older friends. They all feel it helps a great deal to dull the shock of the truth. When someone says, "Happy birthday and many happy returns of the day," I usually say, "If God takes up my option." In the motion picture business there were once options, usually yearly. If taken up, your contract was extended for another year by the studio. It is appalling to realize that God has taken up my option for seventy-eight years.

Kath kept wanting to know what I wanted for my seventy-sixth birthday. I always replied, "Seventy-six trombones." On my birthday, she asked if she could plan what I wore, without any questions from me. Thinking it was a cute idea, I agreed. Her father had given me a USC sweatshirt for Christmas, and she asked me to wear it. Can you imagine my surprise when I heard music outside the apartment house where I lived?

I looked down from the terrace, and there to my wonderment was the Trojan band of the University of Southern California. Their uniforms were impeccable and they marched with such precision, all trombones playing the famous song from *The Music Man*—"Seventy-six Trombones." What a birthday! They also played "Happy Birthday" and performed a well-rehearsed routine in my honor.

After they finished, I went down and shook hands with one and all. It was the first time I had been out of the apartment since my return from New York. Looking up at the apartment house, I saw that every window was filled with people—partly, I'm sure, in surprise at seeing me after such a long time, but mostly to applaud the wonderful USC Trojan band. I took it for granted that this was Kath's birthday present to me, but as I hugged her she told me it was a present also from Harold Schiff.

My most awesome experience during the eighties was the result of an interview in *Playboy* magazine. For what reason I cannot imagine, I mentioned that as a teenager I had posed in the nude for a statue of Spring, by a sculptress in Boston, and as far as I knew it was still in a park somewhere in the city. The rest of what I said to the interviewer was that the sculptress was an elderly woman with a male assistant. She had a little dressing room at the top of a flight of stairs and told me to go up and remove my clothes, please. After fifteen minutes or more, I was still up there when she called out, "Miss Davis, we're ready." I was absolutely panicked . . . but I took off my clothes and there I was. I walked very slowly down the stairs. My face was beet red, I'm sure, with embarrassment.

To my astonishment, this started a city-wide search in Boston that lasted for months. *Playboy* carried a follow-up story in its next editions. Newspapers around the country gave it front-page-type attention, and the *Boston Herald American* ran a headline that asked: "Can You Find Bette Davis' Nude Statue?" On an inside page appeared photographs of three nude or seminude statues in Boston city parks. The caption asked: "Is one of these Bette?"

Finally the statue was found. It was privately owned by a man who lived on an estate in Belmont, Massachusetts. Sculpted in bronze by Anne Coleman Ladd, it was part of a fountain showing four figures dancing around a circle. It is quite lovely. I had the perfect figure for it. And the innocence—I was sixteen and just out of high school.

I posed for the statue to help earn money to add to my mother's funds. My puritan New England upbringing made the experience a difficult one. Mine was another era, almost another world.

In the same *Playboy* interview, I aroused another furor with a statement of mine, the subject being white wine. I said to the reporter, "I am bored with people who drink bottles of white wine at the cocktail hour and claim they do not drink. They often are far 'tipsier' than any of us who drink scotch and water or vodka and tonic." The result of this remark was a barrage of resentful letters from white-wine drinkers. At parties people would apologize to me for drinking white wine. I have never learned when to shut my mouth. I obviously should have this time.

The laugh is now on me. After my stroke, I was told by my doctors they would prefer that I drink wine spritzers, which have much less alcoholic content than my scotch and water. Seemed to me this was an irony of fate.

On February 14, 1983, I was asked to appear in a benefit show called "The Night of a Hundred Stars." It was presented and taped in Radio City Music Hall in New York. The Hundred Stars turned out to be nearer a thousand, heaven help us. The rehearsal was more like a cocktail party, hugs and kisses by one and all to people all of us had not seen in years. Jimmy Cagney was one of the stars who participated. His first words to me were, "Bette, you still care! Acchh, you care! It's written all over you." True, I still do care about everything, and especially my career. The big things, little things and in-between things. Titles, casting, hair, clothes, makeup, scripts, directors, everything.

I shared a dressing room before the show with Alice Faye (who had flown all the way from Palm Springs to be part of the show), Lillian Gish, June Allyson, Ginger Rogers and Joan Collins. I had never met any of these famous people. I suppose it seems strange to all of you reading this that not all of us know each other. Unless you work with them, or are an avid party-goer in Hollywood, there really is little opportunity to meet other stars.

We were in the dressing room together for three or more hours before our appearance onstage. During that time Miss Collins never stopped brushing her hair or adjusting the dress she "barely" had on. At one point, she asked if she should wear a stole with it. I replied, "Well, if we suggested it, you wouldn't think of wearing it, would you, Miss Collins?"

Alice Faye and I turned out to be people with the same approach to life. We were hysterical watching Lillian Gish, who is definitely from another world, looking at Joan Collins. Probably thinking, just bosoms and hair and no talent. Alice kept saying, over and over, "Why did I leave my barbecue pit to be tortured like this?"

The first award I received in the eighties was from *Woman's Day* magazine, as one of five "Mothers of the Year." The honoree in the journalism category was Pia Lindstrom, by 1980 a successful television newscaster, and the daughter left behind by Ingrid Bergman when she married the Italian director Roberto Rossellini. When I accepted my award, I wasn't entirely joking when I said, "I hope my children agree with your choice."

By now, I have found out my older daughter definitely did not approve of my winning this award.

During the spring of 1981, I was constantly being asked if I had heard the song "Bette Davis Eyes" performed by Kim Carnes, and on its way to becoming the runaway hit of the year. My grandson Ashley thought it a riot that a song about his grandmother's eyes had, for many weeks, been the number-one hit on the rock-and-roll charts. His grandmother agreed with him. It was a riot.

There was a story behind the song. The two women who wrote it, Jackie De Shannon and Donna Weiss, had been trying to sell it for seven years. Miss De Shannon said she had been inspired by the look in my eyes when Paul Henreid handed me a cigarette in *Now, Voyager*.

When I heard the lyrics—"She'll expose you when she snows you/Off your feet with the crumbs that she throws you"—I dashed off a note saying, "How did you know so much about me?"

Of course, I took it as a compliment. Kim, who won a Platinum Record and also a Gold Record for the song, most generously gave me a framed copy of each. They are hanging on the wall of my trophy room.

I was not always asked to appear on shows just to receive an award. I was often asked, because of my name value, to present

B.D. at thirteen, owner
of her first horse, a
quarterhorse named Sally.

B.D. riding her beloved
Sally, photographed on
the driveway in front of
our house on the coast
of Maine.

No need to explain, it's Baby Jane—a role that brought me added fame. And the first time B.D. saw me made up for Jane she said, "Mother, this time you went too far."

Warner Bros. refused to make *Baby Jane*. At the end of the film Jack Warner (on my left) gave a luncheon for Joan and me with Robert Aldrich, as a kind of apology that he had not had faith in a film I was going to make. He also deeply regretted his decision since *Baby Jane* turned out to be a huge success.

B.D. and mother onstage promoting *Baby Jane*. B.D. sang a jazzy version of the song from the movie. I was thrilled that she did it so well. She holds a Baby Jane Doll, given away to someone in the audience who held the winning number on a ticket.

The two B.D.'s arriv-
ing for the Cannes
Film Festival. That
evening she met
Jeremy Hyman.

B.D.'s happiest day,
the day she became
Mrs. Jeremy Hyman.

Grandson Ashley, one year old, visiting his grandmother in
Westport, Connecticut.

Working with R.J. Wagner in the series *To Catch a Thief.* My name for R.J. has always been "beautiful, just beautiful." That he is, inside and out.

Seventieth birthday party for William Wyler, my friend whom I adored not only as a director but also as a person. He is responsible for the fact that I am now referred to as a living legend.

Michael and mother ready to go to church for his wedding. This marriage has lasted twelve years.

Beverly Sills and I were most interested in meeting Mae West, and a dinner party was arranged. It was a fascinating evening.

MGM's welcome to Jimmy Stewart and me. We started working on pilots for a series on the same day.

Ashley and grandmother en route to the river to make mud pies.

An honor to be in the
White House Oval
Office, chatting with
President Carter.

To be
embraced by
Anwar el-Sadat!
Thank God a
photographer
was near.

On the set of *The Disappearance of Aimee*, photographed by that fine actor James Woods, who was also a member of the cast.

The American Film Institute award is for Life Achievement, an awesome phrase. After so many others, this award was the frosting on the cake.

B.D.'s brother and mother on their first visit to the Hyman farm, Ashdown, in Wyalusing, Pennsylvania.

Visiting Ashdown. Ashley adored his new brother, Justin.

My seventieth birthday party: outfitted appropriately all in black; a funeral wreath on the door, which my guests did deplore; by my side Earl Lennon, "a ham of a fan."

Making the film *Death on the Nile* gave me the opportunity to work with Peter Ustinov, David Niven, Maggie Smith, and Angela Lansbury. Anthony Powell was in charge of wardrobe and did a superb job.

an award. I was more than pleased to present an award to Hal Wallis, my super boss at Warner Bros. for many years. When I had finished my presentation speech and given Hal his award, I started to leave the stage, whereupon I heard Mr. Wallis say, "Shouldn't I say something?"

Of course he should say something. Was I embarrassed! I went back to the microphone and said to the audience: "You can see what Hal had to put up with all these years."

Another time I was asked to present an award to Liz Taylor, as Rock Hudson was unable to be the presenter. Liz at that time was doing *The Little Foxes* in the theater where the award ceremony was being held. If memory serves me correctly, as I presented her with the award I said, "From one little fox to another, it is my pleasure to present this award to you, Elizabeth Taylor."

Before flying West to accept the Charles Chaplin Award for Lifetime Achievement, I found a lump in one breast. To say I was in a state of shock is putting it mildly. X rays and doctors later confirmed my suspicions. I had made promises to many other organizations to accept awards in person, and all of these evenings had been planned months ahead, making it impossible for me to go back on my word. The gaiety and the excitement of receiving awards was, of course, lessened by the possibility that I had cancer.

Burt Reynolds and I received the Valentino Award for Best Actor and Best Actress of the year. The Valentino Award is given each year to American performers, through an organization based, curiously, in Italy. The ceremony itself was sponsored by an American agency. A great deal of my depression disappeared that evening, sharing the award with Burt Reynolds. I am a great fan of his. He is almost the only male star with the sex appeal of a Gable or a Cooper.

The "Thalians," headed by Debbie Reynolds, sponsored the dinner, and Miss Reynolds took over the whole evening. It was no longer the Valentino Award for Burt Reynolds and Bette

Davis. The award presentation was finally accomplished the next day (after midnight) at one in the morning.

I also received a Lifetime Achievement Award from American Theatre Arts. This evening was, almost without exception, the best organized, the most flattering to me and my career. A ballet dancer impersonated me, on her toes, at the same time smoking a cigarette. She was terrific. In my behalf, Lew Wasserman presented a $5,000 check to the American Theatre Arts. They asked President Reagan to make a film tape they could show on the night of the dinner. And my favorite beautiful male star, Burt Reynolds, also made a tape that was shown. I must say, even though I am a Democrat, the president's speech touched me very much, as Burt's most certainly did. For those two busy men to take time to tape congratulations for me was most complimentary. The award was presented to me by Jean Stapleton, whose speech brought tears to my eyes and filled me with pride and gratitude for the time she had obviously spent on her remarks. Added to all this, the presents they had planned for me, including a bound copy of *Life* magazine from years back with my photograph on the cover plus an enormous life story of me inside. The brilliant man behind it all and head of the American Theatre Arts school is Don Eitner.

An organization called Women in Film gives a luncheon each year and honors three women with its Crystal Awards. I was so proud to be honored the same year as Ruth Gordon and the great film editor Margaret Booth.

I received the Louella Parsons Award from the Women's Press Club, of which I am a lifetime member. The Boston Theatre District Association wanted to present me with an award. As it was impossible for me to go to Boston to accept, I asked my son if he would do it for me. He did, and photographs taken of him that evening make him look like the politician he really is.

*   *   *

I was sent a script, *A Piano for Mrs. Cimino*. I did not like it, but when I was told that George Schaefer, who for years had been responsible for the *Hallmark Hall of Fame*, one of the greatest shows ever on television, was the director, I changed my mind. I had casting approval for the male costar in the film, and I was presented with a list of potential choices. Out of the list I chose Keenan Wynn. I had worked with him years before in the film *Phone Call from a Stranger*. Mr. Schaefer wanted me to see him with this present film in mind. When I opened the door the day he came to see me, I saw, to my horror, that he had a beard and a huge moustache. The very first thing I said was, "Keenan, if you play the man in *Cimino*, all this Santa Claus look will have to be eliminated." Me, always the diplomat. He obviously did not want to go that far, and we parted that day. On the first day of shooting, a smaller moustache and beard had replaced the Santa look. His wife later thanked me; she had been begging him to trim his beard for so long.

Cimino was rehearsed and filmed in Vancouver, Canada. Working with George Schaefer was a delight. Keenan proved to be the perfect choice. My performance, guided by George Schaefer, won me the Monte Carlo Award and I'm proud to say the vote was unanimous. This time Kath and I decided our crew present would be T-shirts. Kath thought that since Kim Carnes was on tour promoting "Bette Davis Eyes," she might have T-shirts advertising the song. We were able to contact Kim on the road. She had the T-shirts, and thank heaven there were enough of them for us to buy.

I very much enjoyed making the television movie *Little Gloria . . . Happy at Last*. Lucy Gutteridge played Gloria and was the image of Gloria Vanderbilt herself. I played the mother of the man Gloria married. My wardrobe, designed by Julie Weiss, was a delight, and so was the chance to work with Christopher Plummer, who played my son. I felt that Glynis Johns, who played the mother of Gloria, was truly divine, and it was such great fun to work again with Angela Lansbury. The advantage in this film was the great cast. The disadvantage was jumping from place to place, from the freezing cold on Long Island to the terrible heat of Palm Beach.

I was honored to be nominated for an Emmy for this performance. Had I won I would have shared the award with Peggy Shannon, for the way she dressed my hair, which added tremendously to the effectiveness of my performance, and with Julie Weiss, whose costumes were so beautiful.

A script called *Right of Way* was given to me by my agent. I definitely did not care about the character I was to play. My director in *Cimino*, George Schaefer, was also reading the script. He had formed a new company with Merrill Karpf and they were interested in producing it. George talked to me at great length, which made me read it again. He had also sent it to Jimmy Stewart to see if he would play my husband. When they told me Jimmy would love to play it, I quickly reread the script. I then agreed to make the film. I found out later that the author, Richard Lees, always had Jimmy Stewart and me in mind while writing it. Mr. Lees was on the set every day of shooting and said over and over, "I will never believe I am hearing my words spoken by you and Jimmy Stewart. My dream certainly has come true."

We filmed *Right of Way* in Los Angeles, mostly on a soundstage, which was heaven for both Jimmy and me. That was the world we were used to—no locations. We rehearsed for ten days on the actual set, which was an award-winning one. It helped our performances substantially, because it was just as described in the script. I don't know how to describe adequately the pleasure of working with Jimmy. He is so unactorish. So always prepared and enthusiastic. So like I am in his approach to working on a film. I felt I had known him for years. I wish I had met him when I was younger. I most definitely

116

would have fallen in love with him. I told him this! He gave me one of those Stewart "slow take" looks.

There were two scenes in which we were in bed together. At this point in my life I dreaded playing them. It had been so long since I had been in bed with a man. I really didn't know how to act. Kath couldn't believe she was seeing me like this. Neither could I. It almost made me giggle. Definitely a second childhood.

One day a Mr. Roy Thorsen called to ask if I would give him permission to plan the evening of the Army Ball, which I had never heard of, to honor me. It is a yearly event. He had been in touch with the Defense Department in Washington for months and was hoping to get permission from all the armed forces to award me the Distinguished Civilian Service Medal, the nation's highest to a civilian and only a very few have ever been given since the birth of our nation. Mr. Thorsen was hoping to get permission from the Defense Department to award me the medal in appreciation for my having founded and run the Hollywood Canteen all during World War II. I was very skeptical that the Defense Department would agree to award me this civilian honor.

On the evening of the ball, I was called for by a marine in dress whites, in a Rolls-Royce, to escort me to the Beverly Hilton Hotel, where the Army Ball was held. When Kath and I arrived at the entrance of the hotel, a red carpet was rolled out and inside stood an archway of servicemen all dressed in full formal uniforms. I was totally overcome when one and all saluted me. At that moment, a military band began to play. I was then escorted to a reception room where a predinner cocktail party was in progress. For the next hour I was introduced to many Army personnel and to my delight was congratulated by many of the actors and actresses who gave so much of their time to the Canteen for the years it was open.

117

At this cocktail party, a photographer asked if I would mind being photographed with Bob Hope. He then asked if I would object to going over to where Mr. Hope was standing. I said, "Not at all," and crossed the room to stand by Mr. Hope, who immediately said, "Well, I see you're wearing Nancy Reagan red tonight." I replied, "I've worn this shade of red, Mr. Hope, since long before Nancy Reagan became First Lady." In actual fact, I was wearing red, white and blue—my jewelry providing the white and blue, diamonds and sapphires. His next charming remark was, "It certainly took them a long time to give you this award. The Hollywood Canteen was forty years ago." I said, "Better late than never. It means even more to me after forty years."

When dinner was announced, I was asked to wait until everyone else was seated in the dining room. After a few moments, my escort, Bob Osborne, and I were taken back into the foyer of the hotel. For the first time, I realized the walls were lined with photographs of me and the Hollywood Canteen. Bagpipes started to play, and I was the last to enter the ballroom. Two lines of pipers formed an aisle for our entrance. When we reached the ballroom everyone was standing as we proceeded to our table. Each step of the way, this fabulous evening left me breathless.

The dining room was a fairyland of flowers, full of many beautiful men in their dress uniforms. It made me realize that the old elegant America still existed. At each place was a gift. For the men, plates with the Army insignia on them, and for the women, crystal perfume bottles. Dinner was served, after which there was super entertainment. The most memorable, praiseworthy event was an enactment of an evening at the Hollywood Canteen, with actors playing servicemen and actresses as hostesses. The sketch brought back many memories of those fantastic years at the Canteen.

My heart had been thumping during all this waiting for the moment when I would receive my medal. The moment finally came. Mr. Marsh, under secretary of the Defense Department, who had flown all the way from Washington to make the presentation, asked me to come up and stand beside him. He said, "This is a medal for meritorious service from 1941 to the present, for contributing to the morale and well-being of millions of servicemen and women. This is the Distinguished Civilian Service Medal, the Defense Department's highest civilian award. This was the unanimous decision of all branches of the armed forces—the Army, Navy, Marines and Air Corps."

Then I was given the beautiful medal. Standing there, looking at it, I wept at this great honor being bestowed on me by my government. Mr. Hope and I were seated at the same table. He was not a happy man. He did not seem to like it very much that this entire superb evening was all in my honor. When we got home, Kath said, "I had always heard about the Hollywood Canteen from you, and now I realize what it entailed. I was so proud of you."

NINE

HOLLYWOOD CANTEEN

THERE ARE FEW ACCOMPLISHMENTS in my life that I am sincerely proud of. The Hollywood Canteen is one of them.

One day just after the start of World War II, in the Green Room, our dining room at Warner Bros., Johnny Garfield sat down at my table during lunch. He had been thinking about the thousands of servicemen who were passing through Hollywood without seeing any movie stars. Garfield said something ought to be done about it. I agreed, and then and there the idea for the Hollywood Canteen was born.

The Canteen was created with that one idea in mind—to give the men in the armed forces a place to meet Hollywood stars. We enlisted the support of the forty-two unions and guilds that made up the motion-picture industry—actors, musicians, carpenters, electricians, writers and so on. We found a building a block off Sunset Boulevard that looked like two New

England barns thrown together. In fact, it had been a little theater and a series of ill-fated nightclubs. We signed a lease for $100 a month for the duration of the war, plus six months.

The first money we raised for the Canteen resulted from a "double ticket," a supper dance at Ciro's after the premiere of a Columbia movie, *Talk of the Town*. The idea came from Robert Taplinger, then the head of publicity at Columbia Pictures. Bob had held the same job at Warners and was to be my loyal friend for thirty-five years, until his death from cancer at sixty. The ticket for the two events was $10, and at the end of the night we had raised $6,500.

At that point the building was only one step below an eyesore. Alfred Ybarra, David Selznick's associate art director, drew up the plans and made sketches and wrangled $2,500 worth of materials. Studio craftsmen did the rest. Carpenters tore out the old floor and walls, with electricians climbing over their backs. Cartoonists drew the murals—gay-ninetyish scenes with a touch of the old frontier. In three weeks these men from the various guilds and unions performed a miracle.

The Hollywood Canteen opened in October 1942. Bleachers were built on each side of the entrance. People paid $100 a seat to watch the first GIs enter, all three thousand of them. This idea came from Jules Stein, the head of Music Corporation of America, who had accepted my request to be the financial adviser for the Canteen. That night the Canteen made $10,000 from the purchase of these seats.

A year later, Warners made a film called *Thank Your Lucky Stars*, starring Eddie Cantor. It was Jules's idea that many of us under contract to Warner Bros. appear in this film doing things that were professionally unusual for us. I sang "They're Either Too Young or Too Old." Among others who appeared were Errol Flynn, Olivia De Havilland, Ida Lupino. At Jules's request, Jack Warner agreed to pay each of us $50,000, which we all willingly agreed to donate to the Canteen. The balance in the Canteen account when we closed was half a million dollars. An organization called the Hollywood Canteen Foundation was formed. The members voted me president. Our purpose was to donate money for worthy projects for servicemen—television sets and swimming pools for hospitals and many more similar things. All this was made possible by the financial genius of Jules Stein. The two other enormous contributions were the free food that Chef Milani urged people to donate, and the enormous effort of Mrs. Jules Stein in providing the Canteen with sufficient dancing hostesses each night during all the years it was open.

The Canteen was in operation for the duration of the war. We finally closed on V-J Day. On any given night a serviceman might dance with Betty Grable to Harry James's band. Betty Grable and Harry James met and fell in love at the Hollywood Canteen and were eventually married. A soldier might ask Hedy Lamarr to pour another cup of coffee, while Marlene Dietrich served sandwiches and Basil Rathbone carried a tray of used dishes back to the kitchen. Each night we averaged two shifts of three thousand men, from 7:00 P.M. to midnight, Monday through Saturday. Some were to be shipped out the next day. Some had just returned from Guadalcanal, Midway or Corregidor, places few of us had heard of a year earlier.

The master of ceremonies might be Eddie Cantor, Fred MacMurray or Bing Crosby. They would ask those who had been there an hour or so to please leave so others could come in. The men never grumbled. There were over thirty-five hundred volunteer dancing hostesses registered with the Canteen. The shows were always on the spur of the moment, never rehearsed. Someone who at nine o'clock was a busboy might be doing a song-and-dance at ten o'clock. Rita Hayworth might be in front of a microphone one minute, behind the snack bar the next. The snack bar ran the length of the building. The dance floor was huge but never seemed big enough for the many who

125

used it. Gargantuan beams were part of the ceilings, the chandeliers were wagon wheels with kerosene lanterns converted to electricity.

The Canteen employed a paid staff of nine and had six thousand volunteer workers to call upon. Each night a crew of more than a hundred was required, in addition to the hostesses. One crew reported at noon to sweep and dust and rearrange the tables. Another came on at 2:00 P.M. to start making three thousand sandwiches. The hostesses, dishwashers, cloakroom girls, doormen and the rest reported at 7:00 and were relieved at 9:30 P.M. Actually, most of the first shift stayed right on through to midnight.

In the first year I encountered the egos and the politics that were a permanent part of the Hollywood scene. When we first organized the Canteen I appeared before the Victory Committee, made up of some of the town's most powerful stars. This committee was in charge of giving permission for actors to appear in camp shows and the like. I asked for and received permission for the Canteen to call actors and actresses directly without referring each request to the Victory Committee.

After our success had been established, and we had created a certain amount of envy among such groups as the USO and the Navy Wives' organization, I was summoned to a meeting of the Victory Committee and told that this permission was to be withdrawn. I could no longer contact the people we needed without going through the Victory Committee.

I replied that what they were asking would make the Canteen impossible to run. We had to be able to call a Spencer Tracy or a Marlene Dietrich at the last minute and ask him or her to appear that evening. I reminded the committee that an understanding had been reached on this point before we opened. I suggested that they refer to the minutes of that meeting.

The chairman, James Cagney, said that "regrettably, the minutes of that meeting had been lost," so they no longer felt bound by whatever commitment they had made. I rose and said, "Mr. Cagney, ladies and gentlemen, I will give you until tomorrow morning to give me back your original permission. If not, I will have no choice but to close the Canteen. I will so advise the forty-two guilds and unions who are a part of founding the Canteen. I will send a statement to the press if you have not changed your minds by tomorrow morning."

The silence hung like lead as I walked out of the room. The next morning at six I received a telephone call telling me that the committee, having met all night, had agreed to let us continue as we had in the past, calling the stars personally. I was overjoyed at their decision. Now I would not have to close the Canteen and the GIs could continue to meet Hollywood celebrities.

During the Christmas season, watching the faces of GIs trying so hard to be cheerful made all of us die a little. How homesick they all were. One Christmas Eve there was a knock at the kitchen door of the Canteen. I opened it and there stood Bing Crosby and his three very young sons. He grinned at me and said, "I thought maybe we could help out tonight." They sang Christmas carols for the next hour. There was not a dry eye in the Canteen. Bing's sons represented everything the GIs were fighting for—a country without war in the future for little boys like these.

The glamorous Marlene Dietrich one night came straight from the set of *Kismet* covered in gold paint. I had never seen two thousand men screaming in a state of near mass hysteria. Marlene was one of the most generous in the amount of time she spent at the Canteen. Roddy McDowall came night after night, helping us out as a busboy. Mrs. John Ford, the director's wife, was in charge of the kitchen from the night the Canteen opened to the closing night. Saturday was Kay Kyser's night. I cannot remember Kay and his band ever missing one Saturday, even though sometimes it was necessary to fly the band back from some distant engagement.

I tried to be on hand any night when no well-known actor was able to come. As president of the Canteen I introduced any celebrities who were there. One night Yehudi Menuhin, then a very young, very acclaimed violinist, was to entertain. I rehearsed all day, praying that I would not mispronounce his name. At the appointed moment I said to the GIs, "I have the great privilege tonight to introduce a great violinist, Yehudi Manure." I apologized profusely. Fortunately, he forgave me and played his violin in his usual brilliant way.

As the war went on year after year, one could not help but notice the change in the age of the GIs. They were all much younger and less robust. British servicemen looking not more than sixteen years old who were on their way to the South Pacific came to the Canteen.

Each night in the Canteen there were many GIs who came from the South. As president, I refused to have the black GIs put in one section of the Canteen. They were free to mingle with the rest. Why not? The blacks got the same bullets the whites did and therefore should have the same treatment. This was naturally a big potential problem. I was well aware that if a southern white GI danced with a black hostess the Canteen could be in trouble. If an incident occurred the band was instructed to play "The Star-Spangled Banner." We had to resort to that only twice in all the years we operated the Canteen.

The success of the Canteen made me very proud to have been a part of it. To this day I often meet men who tell me they had been to the Hollywood Canteen and what a thrill it was for them to see and talk to Hollywood stars. As a matter of fact, Kathryn's father, Cas Sermak, was one of the men who came to the Hollywood Canteen. It makes me very happy to be thanked so many times in my fan mail for providing a place where servicemen were able to meet Hollywood stars. They often tell me in their letters which stars they met on the evenings they came to the Canteen.

All our efforts during all those years were more than rewarded when I received a medal, forty years later, from my country. Besides the regular medal, they gave me a smaller copy to wear if I wore a bikini. Being reasonably sure I would never wear one, I gave it to Kathryn for the devotion to her job all those years.

TEN

WHAT EVER HAPPENED TO BABY JANE?

FEUD is a Hollywood word, a wildly overused Hollywood word. Did Bette Davis and Joan Crawford ever feud during the filming of *Baby Jane?* No!

Like, dislike—these were not words I applied to Miss Crawford. Until we were cast as the costars of *What Ever Happened to Baby Jane?* I knew her only slightly. Our paths had seldom crossed, even though for three years we had adjoining dressing rooms at Warners. For reasons known only to herself, when she came to Warner Bros. from Metro-Goldwyn-Mayer she had asked for one next to mine.

In truth, I did not know her any better after the film was completed. Twenty years after we had worked together, and half a dozen years after her death, we are still a team in the public's mind. We finished only one film and started another. We did not compete for parts since we were opposing types of actresses. I have never been questioned by an audience, or by

133

the press, without someone asking me about Crawford. What did I think of her? What was she like? How did we get along?

Joan was a pro. She was always punctual, always knew her lines. I will always thank her for giving me the opportunity to play the part of "Baby Jane" Hudson.

From the time Henry Farrell's novel about two sisters, former child actresses living alone in an old Hollywood mansion and hating each other, was published, I kept hearing about it. Friends insisted I should play the title role.

When I was filming *Dangerous* in 1935, I had a crush on my costar, Franchot Tone. Everything about him reflected his elegance, from his name to his manners. He had a great deal going for him, including Miss Joan Crawford. He was madly in love with her. They met each day for lunch. After lunch, he would return to the set, his face covered with lipstick. He made sure we all knew it was Crawford's lipstick. I was jealous, of course.

I won my first Academy Award for my performance in *Dangerous*, in the role of a Broadway star who destroyed herself with booze and drugs. I knew, everyone knew, that it was a "Please forgive us for not giving you the Oscar last year when you should have had it for your performance as Mildred in *Of Human Bondage*." That same year, Crawford and Franchot Tone were married, he being the second of her four husbands. Our marital record was one of the few things we had in common. No surprise there. We were both Aries women.

I had heard a lot about Joan's earlier years. I admired the strength and ambition that propelled her in spite of her background. She was born Lucille Le Sueur, in San Antonio, Texas. Her father ran off with a stripper from a Galveston waterfront bar, leaving behind a wife and two children.

In 1961, I was in a play on Broadway, *The Night of the Iguana*, by Tennessee Williams. One night Joan came backstage to see me and told me she had found a novel with parts in it for both of us: *What Ever Happened to Baby Jane?* She said she had sent it to Robert Aldrich with hopes that he would direct it. He had phoned her from Italy, where he was finishing a film, to say he had acquired the rights to the book. He also thought she and I would be ideal for the two leading parts.

Weeks later, Aldrich flew into New York. We met after the theater at my townhouse on Seventy-eighth Street. The first question I asked was which part I would be playing.

He said, "Jane, of course."

I said, "Good. I just wanted to be sure."

The next question was of a more personal nature. Miss Crawford was famous for developing a "meaningful relationship" with either her male star or her director. She felt these relationships gave her a certain power, and there is no doubt in my mind that they did. I do not know, or care, if she was the sexual athlete others have described. My guess is that she was a very skilled sexual politician.

"Mr. Aldrich," I said, knowing he had made two previous films with Joan, "have you had any, uh, personal relationship with Miss Crawford?"

In the silence that followed, I hastened to add, "You may think this sounds silly, but if you ever had, then you couldn't be fair to both of us while filming *Jane*."

Aldrich understood. He laughed and finally said, "The answer is no . . . not that I didn't have the opportunity."

As the producer-director, one of the challenges of his job was to show no partiality of any kind to either of his two female stars. And he didn't.

The first and nearly overwhelming problem that faced Aldrich was financing the film. By this time the bankers had taken over the motion picture business. Four major companies declined even to read the script. Everywhere Aldrich turned, he ran into roadblocks. In 1962, Joan and I were not considered box-office. We were not *bankable*. "Recast it," Aldrich was told, "get some box-office names, and we'll give you whatever you want. But we won't give you a dime for those 'two old broads.'"

Even Warner Bros., my studio for years, turned him down—a decision that lost them a fortune. Nearly a year later, after the picture had recovered its costs in *one weekend*, I was a guest on the *Tonight Show*. A sympathetic Jack Paar listened to my account of how Aldrich had struggled to raise the money. The studio audience howled when I repeated, with undisguised glee, how the moguls would not invest in those "two old broads." In due time, I received a letter from Joan, telling me never to refer to her as an old broad again.

The project was rescued by Eliot Hyman, head of Seven Arts Productions. After reading the script, he told Aldrich he thought it would make a fabulous movie, and that it *should* be done with Davis and Crawford and that he would finance it.

The film would be shot in one month and previewed within two. The budget was under a million dollars—small by any standards. Before 1960 there were no thirty-million-dollar films. Then came a new and absolutely stupid age of megabucks, in which stars received salaries that once would have financed the costliest epic. I find it outrageous that any actor should receive a million dollars or more for a few days' work.

Joan and I agreed to accept salaries of $50,000, far below our usual standards, plus a percentage of the profits. The film was a roaring success, so we did very well financially. Money aside, what actresses would not have killed for the chance to play such parts?

Baby Jane was a breakthrough in women's pictures. Not in ten years had there been a successful woman's film. Actresses had owned the industry for the previous twenty years and the men were entitled to their turn in the fifties and sixties. By then the world's problems were wars, drugs, crime, political corruption—all the ills that involve men much more than women. And writers write about what is going on in the world. Given that trend, *Baby Jane* was truly a break for both Joan and me.

B.D. was given a small part as the daughter of Jane's neighbor. She had made her screen "debut" at the age of three in a film called *Payment on Demand*. I thought it would be fun for her to see in later years. The same thinking applied to both appearances. There was no thought of a career. B.D. never wanted to be an actress and I was delighted.

I decided to do my own makeup for *Baby Jane*. What I had in mind, no professional makeup man would have dared to put on me. One told me he was afraid that if he did what I wanted, he might never work again. Jane looked like many women one sees on Hollywood Boulevard. In fact, author Henry Farrell patterned the character of Jane after these women. One would presume by the way they looked that they once were actresses, and were now unemployed. I felt Jane never washed her face, just added another layer of makeup each day.

I used a chalk-white base, lots of eye shadow—very black— a cupid's-bow mouth, a beauty mark on my cheek and a bleached blond wig with Mary Pickford curls. Jane always wanted to look like a baby doll, as one realizes from the title.

After three days of shooting, Mr. Aldrich said to me, "You can't wear this makeup. It's too much. It's laughable."

Calmly I said, "Let me see the rushes of the first three days' work." I ordinarily never went to rushes, but this time I realized it was necessary.

When I walked into the projection room, several of the Seven Arts executives were there, including Kenneth Hyman, son of Eliot Hyman and first cousin of Jeremy Hyman, whom B.D. would later marry. I had already fought and won a battle to have *Baby Jane* a black-and-white film. Seven Arts wanted to film it in color. It was a black-and-white story. Color would have made it too pretty. Tragedy should never look pretty.

Seeing the rushes assured me I was right. Back on the set, I said to Mr. Aldrich, "If you change my makeup, you'll have to recast me because if I play Jane I will continue to wear this makeup."

At the end of the week, Aldrich came to me and said, "My

137

God, I've gotten used to it, I guess. Keep the makeup. It's just great."

Where the producers were uneasy about how outrageous I wanted Jane to look, they had a problem of another kind with Joan. It was a constant battle to get her not to look gorgeous. She wanted her hair well dressed, her gowns beautiful and her fingernails with red nail polish. For the part of an invalid who had been cooped up in a room for twenty years, she wanted to look attractive. She was wrong.

I understood why she did not want to look unattractive. She had been famous for her glamour all through the years. And there is no question that the glamour actresses made Hollywood the famous place it is today. The glamorous actresses at that time were Jean Harlow, Rita Hayworth, Joan Crawford, Lana Turner, Hedy Lamarr and, of course, Marilyn Monroe. The nonglamorous types, in which group I included myself, were Hepburn, Tracy, Cagney, Fonda, Bogart. The nonglamorous group were all from the theater and had been brought to Hollywood at the beginning of talking pictures. At present, Hollywood may lament the lack of stars as glamorous as those I have just listed.

Never were there two more opposite performers in a film than Joan Crawford and Bette Davis. On the day we made our tests for *Baby Jane,* Joan came to my dressing room and said, "I do hope my color scheme won't interfere with yours."

"*Color scheme???* Joan, I haven't a speck of color in any dress I wear. Wear any color you want. Besides, it is a black-and-white film."

Gradually, Aldrich convinced Joan to make her character, Blanche, less glamorous. It took him one entire morning to talk her into removing her nail polish for a scene in which she came downstairs with her hand on the railing. She argued with Aldrich: "You have taken everything else away from me. You're not taking away my nail polish."

In her vanity she was consistent. As part of her wardrobe,

Miss Crawford owned three sizes of bosoms. In the famous scene in which she lay on the beach, Joan wore the largest ones. Let's face it, when a woman lies on her back, I don't care how well endowed she is, her bosoms do not stand straight up. And Blanche had supposedly wasted away for twenty years. The scene called for me to fall on top of her. I had the breath almost knocked out of me. It was like falling on two footballs!

At times, I was amused by her. Miss Crawford was just not my kind of actress. One scene called for me to hit her, and as a theatrical trick I knew how to do it without hurting her. All you do is cup your hand as you touch someone, the one being hit throws her head back and the sound is added later. But she had her double play the scene with me. It wasn't easy to play this tense and awkward scene with her stand-in.

It was known that Joan was overly fond of vodka. She continually drank Pepsi-Cola on the set while working. Her fourth husband was the chairman of the board of Pepsi-Cola. Joan spiked her Pepsis with vodka.

The final scene in *Baby Jane* was supposed to be filmed on the beach in Santa Monica, but Joan could not stand the heat of the sun at the beach. Alcohol in the body exposed to heat makes one perspire freely. So a set had to be built at the studio and tons of sand brought in.

It was in Joan's contract that the stage had to be kept at a certain temperature. Members of the crew wore lumberman's jackets. In southern California. In August. On a soundstage.

She had an obsession about germs and cleanliness. She never in her life registered at a hotel where she did not get down on her hands and knees and scrub the bathroom. Her children were not allowed to walk around the house without white gloves on.

In one scene in *Baby Jane* I had to hand her two pills. At our first rehearsal, I simply walked over and gave the pills to her. I noticed that she just faked taking them and left them in her palm.

"Miss Crawford, you would prefer that I bring these to you in the bottle, wouldn't you?" I suggested.

"Yes, thank you," she said.

She had a deep and gnawing need to be liked, loved, admired, appreciated. She could be touchingly generous. She brought gifts for me to the set and presented them in front of the crew. Each of her directors received a gift at the end of the picture. Otto Preminger once boasted that Joan gave him a set of gold cuff links. Later, he looked around at a cocktail party and noticed five other men wearing identical sets.

When her adopted daughter Christina wrote a devastating book about her mother called *Mommie Dearest*, describing her mistreatment of her children, I attributed such conduct to her drinking. The book was actually about a child's lifelong effort to win the love of her mother, which she never did.

Baby Jane was one of my favorite parts. The whole project was such a delight to me. It made Miss Carwford's whims tolerable. During our first week of shooting, Henry Farrell visited the set and said, "My God, you look just exactly as I pictured Baby Jane." I was delighted. Compliments from authors always mean the most to me.

When I danced on the beach in the famous scene that ends the film, and my face seemed to glow as I twirled up to the ice cream stand, people swore I had changed my makeup. I had not changed a thing. I changed inwardly and it reflected on my face.

To this day I smile when I remember the first time "Jane" drove down Beverly Boulevard in an old Hudson. The expressions on the faces of people in other cars when they saw me were hysterical. Lots of mouths dropped.

The production budget did not allow for process screen work, the technique used when interior car shots are photographed with a screen in the rear of a breakaway auto, with the background flying past. I actually drove around Beverly Hills most of one day with Ernie Haller, our cameraman, curled up in the backseat of the car, shooting over my shoulder, or sprawled across the front fender, camera grinding away.

Baby Jane was a huge success. In less than two weeks the project was in the black, bringing in $1.6 million in rentals. The negative cost had been $825,000. *Baby Jane* would go on to gross nearly ten million dollars.

I was nominated for an Oscar for my performance. Joan did everything she could possibly think of to keep me from winning. She campaigned openly in New York, contacting all the Oscar nominees who were in plays in New York that year. She offered to accept their Oscars if they won and were unable to attend the ceremony. She also contacted all the members of the Academy who lived in New York, requesting that they vote for one of the nominees then on Broadway. Leaving aside the fact that I felt I deserved to win, the rule of thumb was that an Oscar winner usually added at least a million dollars to the box-office receipts of a film. Since Joan and I each had a percentage of the movie, how Medean, how foolish she was to work against my winning.

I wanted so much to be the first to win three Academy Awards. B.D. and Michael came that night. It was the first time they had attended an Oscar evening. We were sure I would win.

That year, each nominee sat in a separate dressing room backstage, equipped with a TV monitor. I was with my publicity man, and Michael and B.D. were out front. When Anne Bancroft's name was announced, I am sure I turned white. Moments later, Crawford floated down the hall, past my door. I will never forget the look she gave me. It was triumphant.

The look clearly said, *you didn't win and I am elated!*

Joan traveled around the world, carrying the Bancroft Oscar with her. When she came back to New York, she threw a lavish party on the stage of *Mother Courage*, the play Anne Bancroft was in, and presented her with the Oscar.

A year after I lost the Oscar, I was offered another part in a Robert Aldrich movie—costarring Joan Crawford. I told him I would not work with Joan again. The film was originally called *What Ever Happened to Cousin Charlotte?*—a title I very much opposed. I don't believe in repeating successful titles and this was clearly a copy of *What Ever Happened to Baby Jane?*

Aldrich felt a duplication of the title would ensure the success of *Charlotte*. Then came the day when Aldrich stopped by my home to propose that I accept Miss Crawford as my costar. I did not consider this one of his brighter ideas—she was wrong for the part—and I am sure the expression on my face reflected my feelings. Quickly he said, "I don't want your answer right now. Think about it for a day or two."

I said, "I don't have to wait to give you my answer, but if that is your wish I will let you know."

Two days later, I called and echoed his own words: "I don't want your answer right now, Robert, I will accept Crawford, if you will change the title to *Hush . . . Hush, Sweet Charlotte.*" This title was the name of a love song in the picture.

Mr. Aldrich did not give in gladly. Days went by without my hearing from him. Finally, I got the title . . . I also got Miss Crawford.

As fate would have it, she became ill early in the film, an indefinite kind of illness, and checked into a hospital. Weeks passed. The rest of the cast and I kept up with her condition by reading Hedda Hopper, who received frequent bulletins from Joan's hospital room. She had clothes fitted every day. The Brown Derby catered her food.

Her recovery was a slow one, for reasons that I suspected were not entirely medical. She knew I was not likely to be friendly to her, as I had been during *Baby Jane*. Not after helping me lose the Oscar. Also, Agnes Moorehead and Joseph Cotten were in the cast this time, not just I.

She convinced the insurance people she would be unable to return to the film. The crew did not exactly react to this news with despair. For a weekend with *Charlotte* in Baton Rouge, Louisiana, she brought ten suitcases. All her clothes were chiffon and in the heat had to be constantly pressed. She also brought mounds of hairpieces.

Maggie Donovan, who had been my hairdresser for years, was now head of the hairdressing department at Fox. One day she said to me, "We're up to our asses in Crawford's hairpieces."

Aldrich now had to find a replacement for Joan, and his first choice was Vivien Leigh. I objected on two grounds: (1) She was British, and (2) I felt she would be as temperamental as Joan. I told Aldrich this would be like jumping from the frying pan into the fire.

Eventually, he asked my opinion of Olivia De Havilland. I thought she would be wonderful in the part. And off he went to France, where he tracked down Olivia on a holiday in a secluded resort. She took the script to her hotel room and read it overnight. In the morning she turned him down: no, absolutely, no. The overseas operators were busy that day. Aldrich called me. Then Olivia called me. She just did not want to play a villainess.

I begged her to reconsider. "Livvie, you must," I said. "You would be wonderful in this." The next day, she told Aldrich she had reread the script, had talked with me, and would do the part. Which meant that she had to leave for the United States almost immediately. When her plane landed in California at two or three o'clock in the morning—the Paris flights always get in at peculiar times—I was at the airport to meet her.

After a delay of nearly three months, we started over again with *Hush . . . Hush, Sweet Charlotte*. As I knew she would be, Olivia was wonderful in the film.

I must admit, the public liked the movie more than I did. Aldrich was an interesting man, the black sheep of a family as deeply rooted in Boston history as the Cabots and the Lowells.

He is dead now, sadly. I was fond of Robert and enjoyed being directed by him, but he had strange lapses of taste. I thought the scene in *Charlotte* in which the head bounces down the stairs was a bit much. *Baby Jane* had some shocks and high drama, but no heads bouncing down the stairs.

To this day, I think of *Baby Jane* as the picture that caused me to give up driving a car. The day of the ice cream scene on the beach, B.D. and I left our motel in Malibu and drove onto the Pacific Coast Highway to go to the location for the beach scene. I did not angle the car enough on the crossover. A woman came barreling down the highway at eighty miles an hour.

B.D. was singing, "When the red, red robin comes bob-bob-bobbing along." She suddenly stopped. God—I looked and she was all right. The woman slammed on her brakes, skidded, and rammed into the rear end of my car. She was not hurt, nor were B.D. and I, but we were badly frightened. I loved driving a car. After that experience I should have started driving again immediately, but I didn't. Now with the madness of the freeways you could not pay me to drive again.

In May 1963, B.D. and I were invited by Mr. Aldrich to go to London to promote *Baby Jane,* and then on to the Cannes Film Festival, where I would see the film for the first time.

At the festival, B.D. met the man who eventually became her husband. For many years afterward—or, at least, months that seemed like years—I wondered what I could have done or not done. I could have not taken her to the Cannes festival. It's that simple. We had been told that Jeremy Hyman of Seven Arts was to be B.D.'s escort to the showing of the film that evening. Jeremy had been asked by his boss, who happened to be his uncle, to escort Bette Davis's sixteen-year-old daughter to the showing that night. He was livid. At thirty he didn't relish the role of baby-sitter. On the other hand, B.D. and I thought Jeremy Hyman would be the typical fat-old-Hollywood-producer type with a cigar in his mouth.

When I opened the door of our suite at the Carlton, our hotel, there stood an attractive young man. He said, "I am Jeremy Hyman. I have come to escort Miss Sherry to the showing tonight." B.D. and I looked at each other . . . he was not a fat-old-Hollywood-producer type with a cigar in his mouth. I could tell by the way Jeremy was looked at B.D. that he was very surprised and pleased that she in no way looked like a sixteen-year-old needing a baby-sitter. She was smiling at him and something was happening, but in the rush and excitement of leaving for the theater, I forgot about it.

The lobby of the theater was enormous and elegant, packed with cheering fans. When Robert Aldrich and I entered, the theater audience was standing as customary. No one sits until the star is seated and no one leaves after the film until the star has left. I was overwhelmed by it all.

I saw the film in its entirety for the first time that night. I always have a negative reaction to myself on the screen. *Baby Jane* was no exception.

B.D. and I had planned on staying away from home for a month while I promoted the picture in London, attended the festival, and then vacationed a while longer. After the festival we went to Paris for a week or so, and Jeremy soon followed. There is not a more romantic city than Paris when two people are falling in love. Cannes turned out to be my enemy and Paris wasn't helping my cause at all.

After a week, Jeremy went home to London. B.D. and I also went to London, as I had business there. Another city not helping my cause.

ELEVEN

SONS AND DAUGHTERS

I HAVE KNOWN HURTS OF LOVE, but this was a hurt I found almost impossible to handle. B.D. was a person as well as a daughter I adored. I took it for granted she would be with me at least until she was twenty-one. A great part of my life had been more livable because of her. How could I have ever expected that she would find, at sixteen, the man she wanted to marry?

To compound my distress, the man she loved was an Englishman. I love England and its people. I have many English friends. I have often noticed how English husbands order their wives around. English women seem to accept it. So did B.D. In this area Jeremy proved to be a typical English husband. Jeremy and I often said that we would have lasted five minutes as husband and wife.

During our stay in London I wrestled with the fear that if B.D. decided to marry Jeremy I would not be able to stop her.

She was in love and was a girl who knew her own mind. She was always older than her years and boys her own age bored her. When she married Jeremy he was thirty.

There is a wonderful moment in a young girl's life, when she stands unsteadily in front of a mirror, wearing her first pair of high heels, and discovers she is pretty. She may never feel the same assurance again, but it doesn't matter. She has crossed the line. B.D. crossed the line at fourteen. I remember this happening to me at sixteen.

After we returned to California, B.D. missed Jeremy hopelessly. I gave her permission to call him in London often. Expensively often, I might add. This kept her sanity, she said.

Some months later, I accepted a part in a film to be made in Italy. The name of the film was *The Empty Canvas*. Empty it was. B.D. and I flew to London, en route to Italy, so she could see Jeremy before I started the film. Jeremy's mother was very upset that her only son wanted to marry the daughter of an actress. While we were there we met her, and we were very nervous that she might not approve of her son's choice. Jeremy told us later she found B.D. a delight. We thanked God! During this stay in London, I had hoped B.D. would tire of Jeremy under the ordinary circumstances of his going to work each day, without the glamour of Paris or Cannes. A futile hope on my part. She loved him more with each passing day. It was painfully apparent to me.

B.D. did not want to leave Jeremy and go to Italy with me, naturally. While in Italy, she had an attack of appendicitis. She insisted on being operated on in London, naturally. My secretary, Viola Rubber, went to London as her chaperone and to be with her during the surgery. It was difficult for me to stay behind. I had to finish the film.

Later I was able to join B.D. in London. Eventually we returned to California. By the time we flew home, Jeremy had proposed and B.D. had accepted. Again . . . ditto . . . naturally. A month or so after our return, Jeremy came to California, bringing with him a beautiful pear-shaped diamond engagement ring and a pearl necklace as his present to his future bride. I gave them an engagement party at the Bel Air Hotel. I wanted B.D.'s and my friends to meet Jeremy. While he was with us, we made plans for the wedding and decided on a date. As B.D. was a minor, I would have to sign a paper giving her permission to marry. This I did with great reluctance, but felt if the marriage failed she would, I hoped, have had a rewarding experience. B.D. married Jeremy Hyman on January 4, 1964, in the Episcopal church in Beverly Hills. She had always dreamed about having a formal wedding. She designed her own gown. It was made by Stella, of I. Magnin, under the guidance of Strauser, my saleslady and friend. She also helped B.D. choose her trousseau. The veil was of handmade lace from Marseilles. The material of her wedding dress was white cotton velvet. It was sleeveless, with a high-necked guimpe. A dress very suitable for a bride of sixteen years.

B.D.'s bridal party consisted of five bridesmaids, all second cousins, the Favour girls. Her maid of honor was Faye, Bobby's daughter. Her ten-year-old brother Michael was the ring bearer. Jeremy's family flew to California for the wedding. They were all from New York City or London. They stayed at the Bel Air Hotel, a short distance from my home on Stone Canyon.

The church was decorated with sprays of pine and pink carnations at the end of each pew. B.D.'s favorite color had always been pink. Many, many lighted candles gave the church a most romantic atmosphere. Chimes rang as they became man and wife. Jeremy was overcome by the beauty of the chimes, which gave him and B.D. a joyous feeling about the future of their life together.

B.D. had chosen to come down the aisle without someone's arm to lean on. As there was no father available, she did it on her own. So, all five feet, eleven inches of her stood so erect,

151

resembling the figurehead of a ship, with a broad smile on her face. She looked so beautiful and happy walking toward the man she loved who waited for her at the end of the aisle. I promised myself I would block out the fact that when B.D. took that walk she was already *married*, as I will explain later.

When the ceremony was over, the new Mrs. Jeremy Hyman, stepping down from the altar, preparing to leave the church, winked at me devilishly, much as to say, "We did it."

As B.D. and Jeremy exited from the church, I left through a back door very quietly so as not to be photographed with them by the many members of the press waiting outside. I felt this should be their moment, and I was sure they preferred no help from a famous mother/mother-in-law.

The reception was held at the Beverly Wilshire Hotel. I shocked one and all by not having a receiving line. I found it totally unnecessary for the bride and groom to go through this ordeal, as everyone knew each other. At some point, I realized that I had not introduced B.D.'s mother-in-law, Dorothy Hyman. Hoping to make up for this, I escorted her from table to table, introducing her to our friends. I received an enthusiastic hug the next day from my son-in-law for not making him stand in a reception line. The wedding cake was oohed and aahed at by all present. The bride and groom were toasted with champagne, Dom Perignon, the groom's favorite. I don't remember exactly what I said when I toasted them. I vaguely recall that I forgave him for taking B.D. away from me and hoped she would make him a good wife. The bridal couple danced the first dance, of course. B.D. asked the orchestra to play a rock-and-roll number, for which she took off her veil, to the amusement of all the guests. The hit of the evening, however, was her ten-year-old brother dancing with her ten-year-old bridesmaid, Pamela Favour. Her brother was wearing his first tuxedo.

They spent their wedding night at the Beverly Hills Hotel,

which I managed to keep a secret so they were not disturbed. I went to their rooms earlier on the day of the wedding and put iced tea in the scotch bottle, Scotch tape on all the faucet openings, and black satin sheets on the bed. Jeremy had once mentioned that he thought black satin sheets were the sexiest background for a roll in the hay. I must say they were hard to come by for a king-size bed, but find them I did. My new son-in-law obviously had extravagant tastes, Dom Perignon and black satin sheets included. Of course, champagne was waiting for them in a cooler, along with masses of flowers.

That night, after the wedding I returned home in a daze, with no "father of the bride" to console me. I have never up to then, or since, felt so alone. I couldn't sleep. I spent the night stretched out on my huge chaise lounge in the living room, chain-smoking, looking off into space. B.D. has always been a noisy, chatty person, just like her mother. She filled whatever room she was in with energy. She would come bursting home after a date to tell me all about it. She will never come home again any night. She was a married lady, with her own life to live. Her husband was now her priority, which is as it should be. I miss B.D. every day of my life. I always will.

The day after the wedding, B.D. and Jeremy flew to New York to his apartment, where they lived for the next few years. His business interests did not give him time for a honeymoon. I was very proud that if she felt any disappointment, B.D. never showed it or talked about it. I, of course, was sick about her missing a most important part of being a bride. The honeymoon.

Months later, I wrote the lyrics to a song that described my thoughts and feelings while attending her wedding. The song was included in an album I made in England, under the brilliant guidance of Norman Newell, which was released in 1983 in the United States. The title could only have been:

MOTHER OF THE BRIDE

Here comes the bride down the aisle
All dressed in white see her smile
May she be happy all of her life
May she make him a wonderful wife.

Here comes the bride
Here comes my little girl
Oh, I know she's all grown-up
Taller than I am
Even talks back to me
I just can't picture her married

She's been the comfort of my life
What shall I do without her?
Oh, she looks so beautiful and so young
Why must she leave me so soon?
Haven't I always been a good mother to her?

Haven't I done everything
   in the world for her?
Did I do all those things, spend all
   those years, only to lose her?

Oh, I know he's a fine boy,
   bright, well mannered, nice-looking,
   anxious to make something of himself
But he's obviously not good enough for her.

Here comes the groom
Filled with pride
Standing so tall by her side
Friends and relations are crying for joy
Touched by the love of a girl and a boy.

People say you don't lose a daughter
You gain a son; nonsense, I'm losing
   her and I know it

Maybe it's selfish of me to feel this way
But what can I do?

I carried her, I diapered her,
I cared for her, I worried about her,
I scolded her, I spanked her,
I loved her, I loved her
And I don't want to lose her.

Why am I carrying on so?
It may be worth it to just
    get those rock-and-roll records
    out of the house
And I was even learning to like them.

Maybe I will have some peace
    and quiet for a change
No more noise
No more giggling girlfriends
No more eager-beaver boyfriends
No more stories of
    who broke her heart this week
No more three-and-a-half-hour telephone calls
No more . . .

Don't wait up for me, Mummy,
I'll be home late tonight
My little girl
Won't be home late tonight
She won't be coming home at all
Any night.

Here comes the bride down the aisle
All dressed in white see her smile
May she be happy all of her life
May she make him a wonderful wife.

That night after the wedding, I realized I was no longer the "mother of the bride." With a certain amount of fear, I realized

I was now part of that timeless American stereotype, a *mother-in-law*. You know the image: a battle-axe, with one eye in the middle of her forehead, and carrying a broomstick. I was determined to be the other kind, the one who behaves more like Mary Worth than Ma Kettle. Who is there when she is needed, when the baby is sick or the car breaks down, and who probably knows more about settling an argument, or staying out of one, than the secretary of state.

But the lyrics of the song echoed in my head: *You don't lose a daughter, You gain a son.* I *was* losing a daughter, but not, it soon became obvious, gaining a son. My first inkling of this had come earlier, when Jeremy persuaded B.D. to become his wife in a civil ceremony in our home, a week earlier than the date on the invitations that had already been printed. When B.D. told me of the change, she said Jeremy wanted to marry before the end of the year for tax purposes.

We had to change the date on our beautiful pink-bordered invitations, not only spoiling the look, but making B.D. and me seem totally disorganized as to when this wedding was supposed to take place. I asked Jeremy, years later, how much he had saved in taxes with the new wedding date. Three thousand, he said.

I said, "My God, Jeremy, I'd have given you a check for that in five minutes flat to avoid the heartbreak of knowing that when my daughter walked down the aisle of the church she was already married!"

In the weeks after the ceremonies, I thought very often of Jeremy's request to change the date of the wedding for tax reasons, and of the fact that B.D. had had no honeymoon. (I have never been able to believe that this was not a huge disappointment to her.) But I must admit that in these and other occurrences, B.D. happily acquiesced. I was upset for her, and by her. From the beginning, she did whatever Jeremy told her to do. B.D. was a daughter who knew her mother well. She was

156

discerning enough to know how sad and hurt I would be by both these decisions.

I remember very well when we were all in Paris and they were falling in love after the Cannes Film Festival. We had a suite at the Crillon, with a huge terrace off the bedroom. They were having breakfast there one morning. I was puzzled at not hearing B.D.'s voice, as Jeremy kept talking and talking. Later I said, "B.D., when are you going to be allowed to express an opinion?" She sort of muttered, "Oh, he's different when we're alone. He lets me talk."

As the years went by, he never did. This continually infuriated me. The B.D. I knew would never have allowed anyone to make decisions for her. But as this inequity did not seem to disturb her, I had to accept it as a mother-in-law and a good one, as I honestly feel I have been.

I missed her so terribly! On their first anniversary I sent them a dozen white roses. The second year, two dozen, and so on, each year. By their fifth anniversary I said, "From now on you get only one dozen roses no matter how many years." The Hymans had obviously made it.

That first year without her was a desperate time for me. Jeremy was clearly afraid that this famous mother-in-law would not let go of her sixteen-year-old. B.D. went out of her way to prove that she needed a husband, not a mummy, and that I was a thing of the past. This quarantine lasted nearly three years.

After a few years in New York, Jeremy bought B.D. a house in Weston, Connecticut. I was making a film in England at the time. During a telephone conversation with me while I was there, B.D. suddenly asked me if I would like her to find me a house in the area. I was thrilled. For some time I had wanted to move back to New England. And, obviously, the "quarantine" was over. To be living near B.D., to be able to see her every now and then, I knew I had to be a considerate mother-in-law, and not expect to see her very often.

157

She did find me a house nearby, in Westport. I told her to call Harold Schiff and tell him, as I was sure he would want to see it. The day I arrived from England, she met me at the airport and drove me immediately to my new home. It was beside a river and was the perfect size for me and Michael, who was then in school in Chapel Hill, North Carolina. I was so glad to have a home available for him once more, for holidays and vacations from college. I named my new home Twin Bridges, as there was a double bridge nearby over the river. I was deliriously happy to be back in my beloved New England. To be seeing B.D. whenever possible, and having Michael living in a house with me. It was sensational feeling like a mother again.

Soon after my arrival in Westport, B.D. was pregnant for the first time. She had been so impatient waiting for a child. She gave birth to a baby boy on June 19, 1969. He was named J. Ashley Hyman. A happier mother and grandmother never existed. I was so thrilled for B.D., who had waited five years for her first child.

But this joyful moment was not without its measure of pain. B.D. was told by Jeremy to inform me that I was not wanted at the hospital when the baby was born. She did as she was told once again. This obedience to Jeremy has never changed throughout the years. And while I did not ever ask for the same consideration she gave her husband, I did hope that every now and then she would say, "I can't do this to Mother."

I am not sure if it is fear or jealousy that makes a son-in-law feel threatened if his wife and her mother have a close relationship. Once when I was invited to dinner, I expressed delight in a meal B.D. had prepared. The next day B.D. asked me not to ever compliment her in front of her husband. I found this odd. I have never figured out why it would offend Jeremy. I am one who believes in compliments, and regard this practice as one of the reasons my children are so secure as adults.

During the years I lived in Connecticut, I got to know my

first grandson. When Ashley was two years old I was given permission by B.D. to have him spend one day a week with me. His favorite pastime on these visits was making mud pies at the river's edge. How could I possibly have known that this little boy, covered in mud, would one day be in a film with me? His favorite lunch on these visits was chicken drumsticks and French fries.

Ashley was always a joy when he visited me, proving that B.D. was a super mother. She had long ago proven that she was a super wife, which had been my wish for her. We often shopped together, and each Christmas we went into the woods for greenery together. B.D. always made her own Christmas wreaths and pine roping for the stair railings. B.D.'s decorating efforts inside her house were truly works of art. Her color schemes, curtains, rugs, furniture arrangements, made it a warm, inviting home, loved by all who visited her, including her mother and brother.

Some years later, B.D. and Jeremy decided life in Weston was not for them. They started a long search for a farm in Pennsylvania. They finally found one in a town called Laceyville, in an area called the Endless Mountains. I asked the Hymans, only half-seriously, "To what lengths are you going to eliminate me as a neighbor?"

The Hymans completely redid the farmhouse, and it was soon as attractive inside as the Weston house had been. Again, B.D. was the decorator. I immodestly say my daughter is a genius as an interior decorator.

In their second year in Pennsylvania, to her utter amazement and thrill, B.D. was pregnant again. She gave birth to another boy on August 7, 1977, Justin Roger Hyman. I had prayed for a granddaughter. I had hoped she would have the joy of bringing up a daughter, as I had.

B.D. and Jeremy had enjoyed a pool at their home in Weston. I decided to make them a gift of one at the farm. Jeremy did not often thank me for additions to his home. He did thank me for the pool, however, remarking that when he came in from haying, it saved his life to be able to cool off with a swim. The happiness that these additions gave to B.D. repaid me a hundredfold.

I made a decision years earlier that was contrary to the usual behavior of parents after their children marry. I made a gift to B.D. of many pieces of furniture that had been in her homes from the time she was a little girl. I have never approved of parents making their children wait until their demise to give them things that could give them pleasure at an age when they might better enjoy them. I am doing the same for Michael.

My house in Westport was on a road called Crooked Mile. Interestingly enough, Jeremy and his mother had lived on this same road during World War II. Many people from Great Britain, especially if they had children, came to America in those troubled years. What a strange quirk of fate that B.D. would find me a house at the other end of the road from where her future husband lived as a little boy.

Also on Crooked Mile lived a girl called Chou-Chou. More and more I observed Michael leaving the house and walking down the road. Being the quiet type, Michael did not give me any explanation about where he was going. I strongly suspected it had to do with a girl. In his last two years of college he drove home more and more on weekends. The trip from Chapel Hill to Westport was 600 miles. I worried, of course, that he was neglecting his studies. I accused him of being in love with Chou. He admitted it. He said he wanted to marry her.

Michael had decided to go to law school after his graduation from college. I was delighted he had made a choice for his future. I then urged him to give up any idea of marriage until he had finished law school. As is usually the way with parental advice, he did not take it. A few months later, Michael proposed to Chou-Chou and she accepted. I always promised him one of my rings as an engagement ring when the time came, and this he gave to Chou.

Autographing my first LP record, *Miss Bette Davis Sings*.
I was thrilled so many people came. *(Photo © by Robert Scott)*

As the mother in *Strangers*: proof beyond a doubt that my appearance on the screen was always based on the reality of how the character would look in reality.

Gena Rowlands, my costar in *Strangers*, for which I won an Emmy. We were photographed for publicity "out of character," looking as we really did.

Being interviewed by Mike Wallace for *60 Minutes*. He also interviewed B.D. and Michael. *(Photo courtesy of Lester Glassner)*

Skyward was filmed in Dallas, when temperatures were often over 110 degrees. I found Ron Howard to be an excellent director.

With Kim Carnes, singer of the hit song "Bette Davis Eyes," toasting each other. It was a thrill to become a part of the rock generation. And Ashley told me "I had finally made it."
(Photo © by Mark Sennet)

A nervous experience but a rewarding one, working with Ashley in his first appearance as an actor in *Family Reunion*. He was unbelievably good, from the word go.

With the help of my director George Schaefer, my performance in *A Piano for Mrs. Cimino* was one of my best.

A fabulous evening. For my founding of the Hollywood Canteen, I received the Defense Department's highest award to a civilian.
(Photo courtesy of AP/World Wide Photos)

The pilot for *Hotel* with James Brolin and Connie Sellecca. That was my only appearance in the series, because of my illnesses. In my opinion, a better title for it would have been *Brothel*.

Jimmy Stewart with me in *Right of Way*. A delightful experience costarring with him. I adore him.

The Monte Carlo award for *A Piano for Mrs. Cimino*, received on my seventy-fifth birthday. *(Photo © by Alan Berliner, courtesy of Gamma-Liaison)*

Seventy-five and still
going strong.

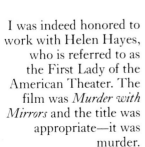

I was indeed honored to
work with Helen Hayes,
who is referred to as
the First Lady of the
American Theater. The
film was *Murder with
Mirrors* and the title was
appropriate—it was
murder.

A photo from my last TV special, *As Summers Die.*

Margot Merrill photographed at the Lochland School, her second
home for many years.

Michael, his wife, Chou, and their first son, Matthew Davis Merrill.
I was delighted they so honored me.

Cameron Merrill,
Michael's second son
and my fourth grandson.

B.D.'s sons, Ashley and Justin, photographed while visiting me in
California for Christmas. What a fantastic present!
(Reprinted with permission from the December 1983 issue of McCall's)

My favorite photograph of Kath. The photographer was the great
George Hurrell.

Harold Schiff, for many years my lawyer, my best friend, and father to my children.

In 1986, at seventy-eight, feeling great and having a ball with
Johnny Carson.

They announced their engagement in April and were married in May, at the Westport Congregational Church. Two dozen of his fraternity brothers drove all the way to Westport from Chapel Hill for the wedding. I thought it was a great compliment to him.

Michael's father, Gary Merrill, came to the wedding. We stood side by side at the head of the reception line. Gary had obviously regained control of his life and was once more the attractive man I had met during the filming of *All About Eve*. I often wished that my feelings toward Gary had been less hostile, and that he had not given me such good reasons for having them.

Now the nest was empty and I wallowed for a time in the sadness of it. The first years of Michael and Chou's marriage were spent near the campus of Boston University Law School. Chou was the principal breadwinner, with Michael taking part-time jobs whenever he could spare time from his studies.

After Michael graduated, he passed the bar exam for Massachusetts. His first job as a lawyer was with the military in Germany, and they lived in Munich for three years. After his return he continued to live in Boston and decided to open his own law firm. I felt this was a very precarious decision, but he has proven me wrong. He now has three or four partners in his firm, and was elected as the youngest selectman in Chestnut Hill, Massachusetts.

The Merrills have two sons. The first was named Matthew Davis Merrill, honoring me with his middle name. In December 1984, a second son, Cameron Snow Merrill, was born. Once more I had high hopes for a girl. I am still waiting, after four grandsons. Michael and Chou now live in their own delightful New England–type house in Chestnut Hill.

In 1982 I rented a house on Long Island for the summer. And on the Fourth of July weekend, I had a family reunion with B.D. and Jeremy and their sons, Ashley and Justin, Michael and Chou and Matthew. It was the first time we had all been together under the same roof for many years. Once again I felt like a mother—cooking three meals a day, planning various activities like croquet, tennis, collecting mussels, which the Hymans especially devoured.

Two weeks before, Kathryn and I started our preparations for the reunion. To put it mildly, the house I had rented was a mess, especially the gardens. We pruned two truckloads of dead branches and weeds and other debris, which cost $125 to have hauled off to the dump. Because of our extensive cleanup of the grounds, we robbed many little mice of their homes. The result was an invasion of these same rodents into our house, which provided hours of unplanned entertainment.

Kathryn painted a dilapidated, rusty set of swings, and window boxes, filling the latter with geraniums in honor of the occasion. We shopped for garden furniture, rafts to use while swimming in the bay, various sizes of beach thongs, beach balls, pails and shovels—all for the children to enjoy.

Dinner for the Fourth was, of course, lobsters, which all of us had learned to love while living in Maine. We managed to have a few fireworks of our own. Added to these was the display of fireworks, contributed by the town of Huntington Bay, which we could see from the house—unbelievably spectacular. It was four days I will always treasure.

After all had departed for their various homes and the excitement was over, for many, many days I was incredibly lonely for all of them. Kathryn and I were also totally exhausted, and quite frankly looking forward to a restful period. Little did we know what was ahead. That night Kathryn woke up in excruciating pain. We could not imagine what was wrong, and we did not have any doctor to contact. Finally at four in the morning I prepared my handbag and got dressed, knowing I would have to call a hospital and send for an ambulance. Kathryn absolutely refused to go. I then called friends who found a doctor to come to our house. The cause of all Kathryn's pain proved to be a kidney stone. I would not wish the agony that

Kathryn went through, or the fright I went through, on my worst enemy. We named the stone Sabrina. After impatiently waiting a week, Sabrina went away. We were then able to take the "overdue" days of rest we so richly deserved after the Fourth of July holiday.

During the visit of B.D. and Michael and their families, I had flashes of memories about bringing them up and wondering if they would run into the same hurdles bringing up their children.

All parents want to be loved. I firmly believe, however, that if your children have never hated you, you have failed as a parent. When B.D. was about seven years old, I accused her of cheating at a game we were playing. She threw herself on the floor, screamed, "I hate you! I hate you!" and stamped her feet in as accurate an impression as one will ever find of a typical Bette Davis scene on the screen. She really did hate me for perhaps half an hour. She then apologized and told me she didn't really mean it. I explained to her that if she cheated in games with her friends, she would keep very few.

I also remember the time that B.D. had been shopping with me and when we got back home she leaned over to pick something up and a small object fell out of her little bosom. She hurriedly picked it up and ran quickly upstairs to her room. I realized it must be something she had taken from a store. I went immediately to discuss this with the children's governess, Coksy. I said, "B.D. is a thief." She laughingly replied, "All children do this at least once in their lives." I went to B.D.'s room, had her show me the object of her "thievery"—a miniature teddy bear—and I then said, "B.D., next time you will have to return to the store and admit you took something." Nothing like it ever occurred again.

From the day B.D. was born, I made up my mind that no child of mine would be brought up in Hollywood. In no way did Hollywood represent the life-style I wanted for her. I felt the same way about Michael and Margot.

163

Margot has been a student at the Lochland School, in Geneva, New York, since she was three years old. As Margot was a brain-injured child, being away at school was a necessary way of life for her. She could not come to the reunion, and we missed her.

Margot is past thirty now. She has come home often, and our times together have been happy. On one of her birthdays, I took her to New York and "pulled out all the stops"—nightclubs, theaters, the works. Wherever we went I was asked for my autograph. In the car going back to the hotel, Margot said, "Mummy, may I have your autograph?" Sometimes you laugh to keep from crying.

For one year, Michael attended a public school in Beverly Hills. I gave him a birthday party and invited his whole class. Michael never got to open any of his presents. His guests were so eager to see what they had given him they beat him to it. During this mad, mad "grabbing" of their presents, which was totally bewildering to him, Michael said, "Mother, I thought these were for me."

I got a clear sense that the mothers who bought the presents were hoping that their sons would give the birthday boy the biggest or most impressive gift. Soon the guests were tearing through the rooms, obviously having been told to report what kind of house Bette Davis lived in. It was the fathers who came to pick up their children at the end of the day, each with a dog on a leash, mostly poodles, or so it seemed. Of course, I felt it necessary to invite them in. Soon there was a swinging cocktail party in progress. That was the last child's birthday party I ever gave in Hollywood.

When Michael went to school the year we moved to Maine, he came home after the first day crying. I never believed that a five-year-old boy should wear long pants, and that day he was wearing shorts. And he was a new boy in school, with hair a beautiful golden blond. All these ingredients were definitely a problem for him. One of the boys called him a sissy and tried to beat him up.

That night we had a long discussion of how he must learn to fight back, with me showing him how it should be done (quite a sight, I'm sure). That lesson, and the wearing of long pants, established him as a regular guy among his new classmates on the second day of school.

It is important that parents help their children to be themselves. It is just as important not to make them appear different from other children in how they dress, behave or whatever, if they are uncomfortable with your demands. I was a strict parent, without question. I had house rules for B.D. and Michael. Often B.D. would say, "But so-and-so is allowed such-and-such." The answer was, "You are not." "Why?" "Because I say so." No long complicated discussion, which often becomes confusing to the young person. For instance, many of B.D.'s girlfriends were allowed to date without chaperones. I felt this was woefully premature at nine or ten, so I gave many parties in Maine for both children. I felt this preferable for B.D., for example, to her sitting in a dark movie house with a boyfriend. When she was in her teens, the custom among her peers was to call a boy and make a date with him. I considered that a very unfeminine thing to do and never permitted B.D. to call a boy for a date. In later years, she told me she was very grateful for this restriction.

Today the primary problem for young people is the fact that the first date usually involves sex. For anyone brought up another way, as many still are, a lot of lonely nights are the result. Should one stand up for one's beliefs or go with the crowd? The latter is what I urged B.D. not to do.

During Michael's college years, the primary problem was marijuana. I could find no excuse for it, or for the parents who ignored how dangerous a habit it was. I flatly stated, "If ever he or a friend indulge in marijuana in my house, they are not

165

welcome in the future." And I made it clear to Michael that no more college tuition would be paid. I feel sad that today there is not much discipline being administered to young people, though many are crying for it.

Strangely enough, while working on this chapter early one morning, looking out a window of the house I was renting in Malibu, I was horrified to see a little girl, alone, running up and down the beach. The waves were high, crashing on the rocks. She could easily have been knocked over by waves or swept up by them and thrown on the rocks. To me this was a typical example of the lack of parental care today! Were her mother and father asleep in their house, not knowing she was gone? Probably.

After my return from Westport to live once more in California, it was a few years before Michael or B.D. could take the time in their busy lives to see my new home in Los Angeles. Michael and Chou were the first. The biggest thrill for Michael during his visit was going to a Los Angeles Dodgers game. He and I have always been ardent Dodgers fans.

A few years later, B.D. and her family visited me for ten days. What a delight to have her in a home of mine again. Their vacation included the anniversary of their wedding so many years before, and I gave them a twentieth-wedding-anniversary party at La Scala, in Beverly Hills. It was a gala evening for me and I hope for them. Sitting on B.D.'s right was Robert Wagner, and on her left was Rock Hudson. She had known both of them during her younger years. Jeremy and B.D. spent the night in a room I had engaged at the Beverly Hills Hotel to commemorate their wedding night.

And so we had come full circle . . . or had we? One of the ironies of being a parent is that you have your children a limited number of years, and you seldom see them. You may seldom hear from them. But the power a child has over you lasts a lifetime.

I am conscious of the fact, writing all this, that there will be many women who have gone through a tortuous time being a mother-in-law, and trying to the best of their ability to let their children run their own lives. It takes a while to learn to become one. The job does not come with a guarantee.

Through four marriages, I inherited many mothers-in-law and fathers-in-law. I very proudly say that I went out of my way to treat the mothers and fathers of the men I married with respect and, as much as possible, with love. I wish I could say the same for my husbands, in their treatment of my mother. I must admit, I loved some in-laws less than others, but they were always welcome in our home.

I ran into a problem in one case, resulting mainly from the attitudes of my own mother. Ruthie was horrified to find out that Sherry's mother ran an elevator in a hotel in San Diego. I felt it was totally admirable of his mother to earn her own living, rather than sit around waiting for her sons to support her.

I urged Gary Merrill, who did not have the best of relationships with his father when we married, to invite him to visit us so I might meet him and his wife, Gary's stepmother.

The most I hoped for from my only son-in-law was that he respect the fact that I was his wife's mother, and that he would try to like me. The latter is not always possible. What you pray to avoid is this: In not winning one, you lose two.

I always had been conscious and considerate of my rights as a mother-in-law from the day B.D. and Jeremy were married. I definitely knew I must always respect their privacy. I settled this problem with myself before she was married, and I would advise any woman facing this peculiar new role to do the same.

No visit of mine to the farm ever lasted longer than two nights or two and a half days. It was my choice to keep my visits short. This should be the recommended behavior for the thoughtful mother-in-law. If I may allow myself to brag a trifle, I never resisted the idea that my son-in-law was the new head of the family. I did everything in my power to accept third place. I believe my friends have meant it when they congratulated me for not interfering in the marriages of my children.

My greatest disappointment has been that neither B.D. nor Jeremy was vocally, at least, appreciative of my efforts in their behalf. I was able, once, to do something that inspired Jeremy to write the only thank-you letter I ever received from him.

He had gone into the trucking business and was pretty desperate during the truckers' strike of 1983. He faced the very real threat of having to sell the farm to stay in business until the strike was over. I knew this prospect would be almost more than B.D. could take. She had worked so hard, inside and out, to make hers such a super home. Fortunately, I was able to help them financially so that Jeremy could save his company and their house. I received from him a handwritten note that said, in part:

> Dear Mudder-in-Law:
>
> Your immense generosity in coming to our aid at a time of such importance to us is enormously appreciated. You saved the day for our business and did wonders for our personal morale.
>
> Jeremy

In the same mail was a letter from B.D. In the nice and descriptive way that was so familiar to me, she mixed her gratitude with a touch of nostalgia that recalled sweeter days.

> Dear Mother,
>
> I walked outside to feed the horses and sled with Justin in the white, fluffy winter and I felt so grateful to you for your generosity. I will never not be indebted to you for helping us through this frightening time and saving our home. I sincerely hope that our boys will look back at their childhoods in Pennsylvania as fondly as I do my childhood in Maine, and that it will stand

them in good stead with a basis of good and real values
as it did Mike and I.

I love you very much.

B.D.

One wonders if she remembers feeling this way, once, way
back then.

TWELVE

B. D.'s FATHERS

I MET WILLIAM GRANT SHERRY, an artist recently out of the Marines, at a party in Laguna Beach. On November 29, 1945, we were married. I justified this dreadful mistake in many ways. I was lonely and restless and had been a widow for two years. These were war years.

If you did not live through that time—the war and the years immediately after—you cannot appreciate how lives were tossed about. I had said *finis* to a romance with a man I thought I might marry. He had been in Europe for the duration and was being transferred from the European theater to Japan, as many were. (It annoys me that zones of war are called "theaters.")

Before he left he asked me to wait for him. I said if that was what he really wanted, he should put a diamond on my finger. Which he did not and, as I knew I would, I grew tired of living my life in a mailbox.

At which point I said yes to Sherry and did the "Dear John"

173

thing. A friend of my ex-beau was with him when he received the letter, and told me he was very upset. I was pleased.

The opposition of my mother and sister was also a factor in my saying yes to Sherry. I was furious when I heard that Bobby had hired a detective to investigate Sherry behind my back. It was as if my family were saying that at the grown-up age of thirty-five I could not make up my own mind. I will accept advice if I ask for it. I can be told something I dislike. I will think about it and, if the person is right, I will usually come around. But I am not very good at being *interfered* with.

Bobby finally told me she had had Sherry investigated and I must not marry him. I refused to read or hear about the report the detective gave her; one can only guess at what it discovered: his temper, his inability to support himself, his desire to marry money. After we were married, a friend said that Sherry had told his Marine buddies in San Diego that his ambition when he left the Marines was to marry a wealthy woman. This information came a little late.

So did the words of his mother. She told me that she wanted to warn me not to marry her son. But she was afraid of him. He was cruel and very strong physically. This too I was told after we were married—not the best time to learn about your new husband's faults.

I admired Sherry's mother, who, rather than be supported by either of her sons, was an elevator operator in a hotel in San Diego. If I had not been so sure that my mother objected to the marriage for the wrong reasons, I might have said no and pleased them both.

Sherry and I seemed to have a lot in common. He was creative. He loved making his home beautiful. He had a gift for finding beauty in paint and wood, which our daughter inherited. His season was the summer. He was a fantastic swimmer. He had the powerful build of a boxer, but when he wanted to be he was a gentle person. He did not always want to be gentle.

Nothing—not infidelity or boredom—can destroy love as

quickly or as completely as the physical abuse of one person by another. It started on our wedding night in a hotel. Something I said or did provoked him. It never took much. He picked up a piece of luggage and threw it at me. Some minutes later, he acted as if nothing had happened.

His anger was blind and unpredictable, and therefore all the more dangerous. There did not have to be a reason with Sherry. Out of the blue, he could become a monster. I might have left him that first year, except that one does not give up easily on a third marriage. I was not eager to admit that I had failed once again in my choice of a husband, with all the inevitable publicity.

After we returned to Laguna Beach from our honeymoon in Mexico, things were still difficult. I did worry that the fault was mine. I spent long hours at the studio while he stayed at home. His paintings were beginning to sell, but not as well as he thought they should. Our marriage was like a small boat caught in a storm. There were occasional calms which helped.

Any thoughts of divorce were put aside when a miracle occurred. I was going to have a baby. I was thirty-nine years old. On May 1, 1947, Barbara Davis Sherry was born at the Santa Ana Hospital, by cesarean section. She weighed seven pounds.

I had bought a house on Wood's Cove in Laguna Beach after finding out I was pregnant. I hoped fatherhood would be good for Sherry and for a time it was. But the cruelty continued. The day after Sherry threw me down the stairs and onto the front lawn, I did not return home from work. I moved into my dressing room at Warners. Actually, it was a two-story apartment planned for me by Perc Westmore, my makeup man and trusted friend. It had a bedroom upstairs, and a living room and a makeup room downstairs.

The perfect setting, I decided, in which to kill myself. I was quite serious. I didn't want to live this way any longer. How could I deal with such a man? I was even afraid to divorce him.

I was not accustomed to being afraid of someone I lived with. I was desperate. I laid out my best nightgown. I planned every detail. The next morning, when I was due on the set at nine o'clock, there would be a dramatic moment when they broke into my dressing room and found me there. And on the set they would whisper . . . *Bette Davis is dead*.

For years I had sometimes taken a sleeping pill when I couldn't sleep. I got out all I had and lined them up on the bedside table. And then I started laughing. I laughed myself silly. I said, "This is ridiculous. This is just not your bag at all." And I put away the pills.

But that day I had been so confused and disturbed I was incapable of thinking straight. At some point I remembered I had a daughter, and I asked myself, could I do that to her? No, I could not.

I reconciled with Sherry after he promised to see an analyst. I left him for good when one evening, for no reason at all, he threw a silver ice bucket at me. I was holding B.D. in my arms. She was six months old. I had told Sherry if he ever showed any violence toward B.D. I would leave him. I did, once and for all.

The day I finished making a film called *The Story of a Divorce*—an appropriate title (later it was changed to *Payment on Demand*)—the cast and crew gave me a surprise party on the set to celebrate my forty-second birthday on April 5, 1950. I was presented with a huge ostrich egg for being "a good egg."

Sherry showed up unexpectedly at the party and got into a fight with two security guards. I had asked them to have him leave. Then Barry Sullivan, my costar in the film, said to Sherry:

"Where's your sense of humor? The cast and crew are giving your wife a birthday party."

Sherry said, "Stay out of it. I don't want to hit you because you have to be photographed tomorrow."

Sullivan said, "Don't let that bother you."

Before he could say anything else, Sherry knocked him
down. Sherry was always jealous of any actor I worked with. He
who complained about being robbed of his independence, who
gave interviews about the problems of having a wife for a
breadwinner, was alarmed at the thought of losing his meal
ticket to another man. He was prepared to go to lengths I didn't
think possible to provide for his present and future comfort.

I also learned from my housekeeper that my husband had
been having an affair with my daughter's nursemaid during the
hours I was off working. He had also enlisted her help in a plan
to kidnap his own child and return her to me for a ransom. My
housekeeper happened to pick up an extension phone one day
and overheard a chilling piece of their conversation. The location of the street. The time. "Bring B.D."

I had bought a small house near the studio so I could spend
more time with B.D. while I was working. Laguna Beach was a
long drive, morning and night. That was where the nursemaid
had talked to Sherry. When the housekeeper called me at the
studio to tell me what was going on, there was no time for
explanations as I bolted from the set and rushed home. For the
next hour and a half, one of my bodyguards threatened,
probed, and grilled her, and not one thing would she admit.

I no longer had a reason, if any ever existed, to delay leaving
Sherry once and for all. I still felt sympathy for him. I had sent
him to analysts, had overlooked so much, all for the sake of a
marriage that meant nothing to him. I hired Jerry Geissler, a
prominent Hollywood attorney, to renew the divorce proceed-
ings I had postponed too long. I hired bodyguards from the
minute I first left him, and obtained a court order to restrain
Sherry from having anything to do with B.D. and me.

Our battles were now legal ones. To be sure Sherry would
give me a divorce, I offered to pay him alimony for a period of
three years. The three years were nearly up when Gary Merrill,
who was by then my husband, wanted to adopt B.D. He tried
to get Sherry's permission. Sherry said for $50,000 he would

give his approval. When we refused, he sued to get custody of her. A judge in Maine, a stern, old-fashioned Yankee judge, threw the case out of court when he learned that Sherry had received alimony from me.

I was running out of patience, if not remedies. I asked my lawyer what options we had left. He suggested I withhold Sherry's last month's alimony check. For that final check, Sherry gave Gary permission to adopt B.D.

Sherry married the nursemaid, had children, and now has grandchildren.

I have always believed that out of the worst experiences some good comes. B.D. was the "good" from my marriage to Sherry.

One of the most haunting moments of my life took place six months after B.D.'s marriage to Jeremy. They were living in an apartment in New York, and I was visiting with her when the phone rang. I heard her say:

"Daddy, darling! How are you?"

I watched her hang up the phone and asked: "B.D., who was that?"

"My father," she said, her voice matter-of-fact.

"Sherry?" I said.

"Yes," she said. "He's in New York."

William Grant Sherry, her father, my ex-husband—neither of us had seen him since B.D. was three years old. He had just rediscovered his daughter, now going on seventeen and a newlywed. She had not thought to tell me that he had gotten her number, had recently been in touch, and was dropping by later that afternoon.

I hesitatingly asked if I could wait until he came. B.D. said, "Of course, Mother." I simply had to see what he looked like, this man I had once loved, who had made such a mess of my feelings that I thought about killing myself. Women with men are babes on a seesaw. Ever and always.

He arrived. There were polite, awkward hellos, hugs and

kisses for B.D., and after long minutes of catch-up chatter Sherry asked if he could talk to me for a moment, alone. We went into another room. He had changed little over the years, which meant that he was still attractive.

He closed the door and said, "I must apologize for how horribly I treated you years ago."

I thanked him and said, "It's water under the bridge. Just forget it."

Then we were all back in the living room, with B.D. perched on the arm of the couch her father and I were sitting on. She looked from one to the other of us and said, "I never thought in my life I would ever again be in the same room with my own father and mother."

As quickly as I could, with whatever grace I could manage, I excused myself and went back to my room at the Plaza Hotel. I never cried as hard, as uncontrollably, as I did then. I wept not for myself or Sherry or the years lost or ruined, but for B.D. and the little girl who once was, and would never be again.

B.D.'s remark was innocent, meaning much more to me than to her. I never wanted to take a father away from his child. I am a devout believer in the ideal union: two parents for every child. Certainly, any mother needs the help of a man in bringing up children. And how you do! But if she must, a mother can do it better alone, I think, than a father. I will always believe one good parent is immeasurably better than two at war.

B.D.'s reunion with her father turned out to be a temporary one. Sherry had become a Jehovah's Witness—to the point of being a fanatic. When the pamphlets and other literature began arriving, she quietly allowed him to slide once more out of her life. I didn't know it then—perhaps she didn't, either—but he may have planted a seed.

In my life, ironies abound. One of the noisiest arguments Sherry and I ever had, and one of the strangest, took place one New Year's Eve. We had rented a house at Lake Arrowhead, taking with us B.D. and the nurse who was to finally become Sherry's wife.

Waiting for midnight, we decided to see a movie, *Twelve O'Clock High*. It was the first time I had seen an actor called Gary Merrill. I thought he was very good and very attractive, and said so, to Sherry's annoyance. By the time we returned home, we were having a colossal fight over Gary, an actor neither of us knew. Sherry was always crazily jealous.

A year passed. I was in the process of divorcing Sherry when I met Gary Merrill for the first time, on the set of *All About Eve*. Gary and I had flown to San Francisco, where *Eve* was to be filmed, with two of the other actors in the cast, Celeste Holm and Hugh Marlowe, in a private plane owned by Darryl Zanuck.

During the flight, Miss Holm raised her voice to be heard above the roar of the propellers and said to Gary, "I wonder what it's going to be like working with the queen bee from Warners?"

"I can tell you one thing," Merrill replied. "It's all going to be over in eight weeks."

Of course, he was wrong. It was not over for ten years, some of them, in the beginning, loving and happy years. But that story sort of typified Gary. He was not the kind of person who got upset if the sun didn't come out.

There is a near perfect time in a person's life, just past forty, I think, when you have outgrown most of the wildness, either the work is going well or you have adjusted your sights, and you are at peace with your private self. The time may come only once, and this was mine.

The last place I expected to find love was on a movie set. I was too aware of the pitfalls, too smart to let the obvious happen. I had vowed never to marry an actor. Then I found myself amending my own rule: I could never marry an actor I did not think had talent, one I did not respect.

Gary had enormous gifts. What he wasted was part of our

defeat, our sadness as a couple. *All About Eve* was at once the cause of our falling in love and our curse. He wanted to believe that I was Margo Channing. I thought he was Bill Sampson, this strong, protective, secure man.

Joe Mankiewicz, who wrote and directed *All About Eve*, gave Margo one of the most descriptive speeches about the problems of an actress growing older. The public, the critics, even friends, thought they saw glimpses of Bette Davis in these lines:

> Funny business, a woman's career. The things you drop on your way up the ladder—so you can move faster—you forget you'll need them when you go back to being a woman. That's one career all females have in common whether we like it or not. Being a woman. Sooner or later, we've got to work at it, no matter what other careers we've had or wanted. And in the last analysis nothing is any good unless you can look up just before dinner—or turn around in bed—and there he is. Without that you're not a woman. You're someone with a French provincial office—or a book full of clippings But you're not a woman. Slow curtain. The end.

This speech did not apply to me. I never needed or wanted the French provincial office. Or the book filled with clippings. I was not Margo Channing, her kind of actress, her kind of glamorous lady. Gary was not Bill Sampson. Our marriage was not a movie.

All About Eve became a cult picture. Edward Albee told me there was a theater in Greenwich Village that kept bringing it back, and you could never hear one word I said because the people in the audience knew every one of my lines and would say them out loud along with me.

Many of my films I would not need more than a sentence to describe, and that only because it is hard to describe a movie in less than a sentence. But *Eve* is the only one I would pick if I needed to prepare a textbook. All the ingredients were there: a brilliant script, perfectly cast and directed, with a chemistry between the leading man and lady that must have been obvious to the entire crew.

In one scene, Bill returned to comfort Margo over a critic's poisonous column. Merrill and I embraced. Mankiewicz separated us by joking, "Cut! Cut! This is not swing and sway with Sammy Kaye."

It was, for the most part, a happy and a charmed set. George Sanders played the part of the critic, Addison. His then wife, Zsa Zsa Gabor, dropped by one day, insisting she needed George to take her shopping. Joe politely informed her, "We're making a f——ing picture, honey," and sent her away.

Trivia fans remember the picture because in it Marilyn Monroe gave her first important performance on the screen. She played a would-be actress described by Addison as "a graduate of the Copacabana School of Acting."

How my luck had changed. I had been offered the role by Darryl Zanuck ten days before the shooting was to begin, after a back injury forced Claudette Colbert out of the cast. Claudette told Mankiewicz, "It's fate. I had to break my back so that Bette could meet Gary Merrill and get the role of a lifetime."

Gary and I were married on July 28, 1950, in Juarez, Mexico. B.D. joined us, at Gary's suggestion, for part of our honeymoon in Maine. I had my three-year-old daughter's hand in mine, walking along the beach one day, with Gary behind us. He studied our legs and our walk and called out, "My God, I've got two of them."

Gary and I were eager to adopt a child. I had been told after B.D.'s birth that at my age I shouldn't take another chance. Within a month we adopted a five-day-old baby girl named Margot (with a *t*). By January 1954, we had added a son, Michael, a golden boy. Now we were five.

That was an idyllic picture destined not to last. What I wrote in *The Lonely Life* rings as true today as it did twenty years ago: "I sensed in Gary my last chance at love and marriage. I wanted these as desperately as ever."

I did not know then that I had entered what I would later call my ten black years. For three of those years I worked very little, the result of two major physical problems. I had to leave *Two's Company* on Broadway to undergo surgery for a condition that was diagnosed as osteomyelitis of the jaw. My recuperation from this operation took many years.

While I recuperated, the Merrill family moved to Maine. Eventually we bought a house by the sea on Cape Elizabeth, just outside Portland, and named it Witch Way. We did not know which way we were going, and a witch was rumored to live there.

I was caught in a cycle that was new to me. The more distant my career seemed, the harder I worked at being a wife and mother, and the shakier my marriage grew. A sure way to lose happiness, I found, is to want it at the expense of everything else.

Gary was mean and unpleasant with B.D., and I was never sure why, except that I felt it was a kind of jealousy having to do with her being "my" child.

Then we found out that our darling Margot was brain damaged. We made the painful but essential decision to send her away to school. We looked into many and finally chose the Lochland School in Geneva, New York. The loss of Margot was a permanent hurt, and a setback to us as a family. Gary's feelings toward B.D. were not improved when Margot—his own first daughter—had to go off to school. When home, he was restless and irritable and not always sober.

I made a film with Gary, *Phone Call from a Stranger*. We rented a house in Los Angeles this time and brought B.D. and Michael with us. The first day in the house, I opened what I thought was a closet door, fell fourteen steps down into the basement, and broke my back. I was out of work for nearly a year. When I was able to work again, Gary and I were broke, so we rented an apartment in the Chateau Marmont in Hollywood. The kitchen contained a total of four pans, a little difficult for cooking. At least once a day, or so it seemed, I would answer a knock at the door and find a bill collector standing there. Some poor young man who would hang his head and stammer, "I hate to do this to you." I would hold out my hand and say, "Quite all right." The children were in Maine with Gary's brother and his wife.

Even when I was well parts were scarce. I have no clear memory now of why, except that the bankers did not consider me to be box-office. Meanwhile, there were taxes and medical bills and family expenses to pay, and the children were in Maine, living well. I have always believed that you should not saddle young children with your financial problems. We never did.

I no longer remember when I became convinced that Gary and I wouldn't make it. But I knew years before I filed for divorce. I think if there had not been children we might have worked it out, each going his own way and being together when we wanted to.

This fourth failure in marriage convinces me I am obviously a complete failure as a wife.

I think Gary and I were very much in love when we married. Once the love bug wears off, as it inevitably does, you are shocked to discover that you really didn't know the object of your affections at all. We know this to be so, even as we repeat the same mistake over and over and over.

Up to a point, Gary was a good drinker. Then he reached and passed that point. His mornings-after were apologetic. We would send roses to whichever hostess he had insulted the night before. I would tell him how much nicer it would have been to have behaved, and then not need to send roses.

Most of all, I resented the waste of his talent. I could tolerate everything else, if he had shown some discipline. I even got used to his mocking me. If I entertained, decorated the house and grounds, prepared a buffet for twenty people, Gary would throw a party of his own the next time I left home, greeting his guests in tennis shoes with no socks, serving beer and cold cuts, and lining up stones for people to sit on.

The joke was on both of us. I loved making a home for him, but he did not at all like that domestic side of me. He wanted me to be Margo Channing.

Gary and I were well aware our marriage "had had it" when we started rehearsals for *The World of Carl Sandburg*. We had contracted to tour a good part of the U.S. with this show. It was a first for both of us—one-night stands, a different city each night with few exceptions. We wanted terribly to cancel our contract, but of course this was impossible. We communicated very seldom except onstage. We toured in a chauffeur-driven car, usually 200 to 300 miles a day. The most difficult moments were those long drives each day with very little to talk about, because of our estrangement. It was not the most pleasant way to live and work, but the show was such a success and such a pleasure to perform, it helped get us through all our personal problems. Gary introduced me to the audience each night as the mother of his three children. You could feel that the audience was touched by this, and it certainly gave the impression that the Merrills indeed had an ideal marriage. I often used to think, what they don't know won't hurt them.

I had always vowed I would never do a show in any theater in Hollywood, as it is truly a town where happiness reigns if the show and the performances aren't good! However, I agreed to do *The World of Carl Sandburg* in Hollywood, the last city of our tour. I felt confident that we would be a success there because we had enthusiastic audiences and the super reviews everywhere we went.

It seemed that all of Hollywood came to opening night at the Huntington Hartford Theatre. I hoped we would give an especially good performance that night. We did. And thank heavens we were received with enthusiasm. At that point my career in films was at a complete standstill—so was Gary's. This fact, of course, made us both doubly nervous being in front of an audience from our own profession. Would they think that our careers had come to a standstill with good reason? My mother, Ruthie, came up from Laguna Beach for the opening night, as did Bobby. Mother's doctor said seeing me once again on top of it all made Mother live ten years longer.

Gary and I were divorced immediately after the tour ended. The next year I toured through the southern states with the Sandburg show. Eventually I went to New York with it, but the show was not as successful there as I had hoped.

Gary was no longer my costar. Neither of us wanted to work together again after our divorce. I'm sure that if Gary had opened in New York with me the show could have had a long run. On our previous tours, the fact that we were married and had three children was a plus for the audience.

Not long after our divorce, I ran into Joe Mankiewicz at a party. For years I had been asking him to write a sequel to *All About Eve*, telling what had happened to Margo and Bill. I said, "You can forget about the sequel, Joe. Gary and I played it and it didn't work."

THIRTEEN

WE MADE IT

NGRID BERGMAN ONCE SAID that the most important things for a long career were good health and a short memory. In a profession that exhausts the strong and tramples the weak, I had survived once more.

A young actress once said to me, "Miss Davis, back in your era, what was it really like in Hollywood?"

I answered a bit testily: "I have no era. I was acting *back then*, and I am still acting. My era will end the day they put me in my grave." On my tombstone should be written: "She did it the hard way." That is an accurate description of my life and my career. I have loved it all and would relish living *almost* all of it over again.

On New Year's Eve there is a Davis family custom of writing a wish for the New Year on a piece of paper and throwing it in the fireplace at midnight. Kath and I did this on New Year's Eve 1983. My wish was that I would make a film in the next year. With each passing month the prospect of my wish coming true was dimmer. But in late September 1984 a script arrived at my house in Malibu. By now my feelings were divided equally between the desire to work again and the fear that I would be unable to make it.

The script was an Agatha Christie story, *Murder with Mirrors*. I read it, thinking, almost hoping, that I wouldn't want to do it. But the more I read the harder it was to resist. The script was good. The part for me was good. I decided to do the film, my *first* since my illnesses. I was in a state of high excitement one minute, and terror the next. Never far from my thoughts were the questions: Could I make the long days on the set? Could I remember the lines?

At the time of my mastectomy, followed so soon by a stroke, most of my doctors felt there was no possible chance I would ever work again. Certainly, when I accepted the script I had no way of knowing if I could make it. I was told that we had two and a half weeks before we left for London, where the picture would be filmed. Strangely enough, I had told Kath that I hoped the first film I made would be in England. It was almost spooky that *Murder with Mirrors* would fulfill this wish. We felt it was a good omen for my return to work. I would be costarring with Helen Hayes and Sir John Mills. I certainly couldn't quarrel about this casting.

Many years before, Helen Hayes, as the First Lady of American Theater, visited the set where I was filming *The Sisters*. I was thrilled when she complimented me on my work.

In two and a half weeks, decisions had to be made about clothes, the proper hairstyle and the proper makeup for the character I was to play. Houses had to be closed and luggage packed.

Before leaving for London we met Alan Shane, the executive producer; Mr. George Eckstein, the writer-producer; and Dick Lowery, the director. In all fairness, I explained to them my fear about making a film. Even though the doctors had advised the insurers of my full recovery, I had no idea how it would affect me to be acting again. They understood. The room was aglow with assurances and understanding. They would take the best care of me.

In the days that I had left I concentrated on learning the entire script, as has always been my custom. I was in torment wondering if I could remember the lines, had the stroke affected my memory? In two weeks I memorized the entire script as easily as I always had.

One day a big limo pulled up in front of my house in Malibu. Kathryn and I realized we were actually on our way to this grand and frightening experience, working again.

We flew to New York on Regent Air; it was the most luxurious flight I had ever had. Across the aisle was Dolly Parton. We had never met. After a few hours in the air, Kathryn told me that Miss Parton had sent a note to our compartment, saying she did not wish to disturb me, but hoped that she might call on me sometime when we were both in California. I went back to where Miss Parton was sitting and told her I'd love a date with her in California.

We spent the night of October 22 in New York and B.D. drove in from her farm in Pennsylvania to say good-bye. It was a gesture that pleased but at the same time puzzled me. She seldom left her farm to visit me and I had seen her just once in the year of my convalescence. That she had volunteered to come to New York to say good-bye made me very happy. Little did I know then that this would, in truth, be good-bye.

All during the flight to London, and well after we landed, I wrestled with my doubts about making this movie. Kathryn, once more, as in the hospital, kept saying, "We'll make it." Without knowing it, I had been "training" for my return to work. I had taken walks on the beach, each day extending the distance. I had climbed stairs and gone swimming every day. All these things had made me so much stronger.

Even the predictable skirmishes that awaited me were in a

way a good sign, an indication that I was back where I belonged. When we arrived in London, I was not given quite as much care or understanding as had been promised. But then I have been in films for over fifty years and that is never a surprise to me. Film companies seldom live up to any promises and in recent years that has changed not at all. In fact, little has changed in any area of filmmaking. The same mistakes are made and the same problems exist.

The woman who was to design my clothes, Jane Robinson, had flown to America and brought her sketches and fabrics to Malibu. She promised me that my complete wardrobe would be finished before I started working on the film. Far from it. There was only one dress ready to wear for my first day of shooting. With every difficult situation there is some humor sprinkled in. On the set I tried on one of the supposedly finished dresses. It hung on me like a sack. Jane Robinson said, "You must have lost weight over the weekend." I gave her a look that would exterminate lice.

The producers refused to pay Peggy Shannon's salary and made little effort to find a replacement. (As it turned out, Peggy could not have come anyway.) Raymond Gow, a top hairstylist in London, was busy on a film so he couldn't be with me. But he found someone for me who turned out to be *terrific*.

The hotel they chose for us was not right so we moved to the Savoy. Kathryn devised an elaborate plan to get our clothes, freshly pressed and hung, from one location to the other without repacking. She had the Savoy send over a hundred of their hangers, made the switch, hung the clothes on the kind of rack you see rolling through the garment district in New York, and asked the head of the production company to supervise moving the clothes to the Savoy personally, as we had to be working that day. Somewhere along the way, they removed everything from the racks, tied them up into a bedsheet, and left them in the room—as wrinkled as when we arrived.

The next day, one of the London tabloids carried an item

that said Bette Davis had moved to the Savoy and had ordered a hundred specially made hangers, even though her role in the movie would last "only a fortnight." It must have been a light news day. I was in London filming a little over a month.

For sheer excitement, nothing could match the studio's travel arrangements. We were filming an hour outside of London. On two consecutive nights, the car taking us back to the hotel broke down in the middle of the thruway. Once the headlights went out. The chauffeur assured us that he could make the remaining twenty or so miles into London without lights. "Not with us," Kath said. She then told him to turn off the thruway and we'd take a taxi into town. He deliberately passed the next exit. Whereupon the car sputtered and stalled in the center lane. In the freezing cold and pouring rain we left the car, knowing it would explode if anyone ran into it. We were rescued a few minutes later by the head of transportation. He told us he just had a "hunch" that he might be needed. What a hunch!

I have had many moments of nervousness in the one hundred or more films I have made. But seldom have I been more nervous—I am not ashamed to admit this—than on my first day of filming for *Murder with Mirrors*. Quite understandably so, I had not worked in almost two years.

With rejoicing we came to the end of the first day of shooting. I had remembered my lines. I was a bit in awe working with Miss Hayes, I must say. And she confided later that she was also uneasy about working with me. So Kath and I went back to the hotel that night with joy in our hearts. I had not made a fool of myself. It had occurred to me often how foolhardy I was to accept a location film in England in the latter part of October. We had many miserable days on the set because of the cold weather.

There are not many real acting scenes in a movie based on a Christie book, and it was true of this one. Miss Hayes's and mine were scheduled for the last day of shooting. I felt this was grossly unfair. It put so much pressure on us. That morning I made a short speech to the crew, suggesting that they not get too excited about the crew party that is always given at the end of a film. I said we might not be able to have one that night. I explained that it was a trifle nerve-wracking to be told the picture would be over if one finished one's scenes. We would try to make it. (Although I thought we might have done a retake or two, if the director had been less schedule-conscious.)

We did have the crew party that night and it was a huge success. It reminded me of the old days, everyone toasting everyone else. All problems forgotten.

There is a perfect moment for an actor, when you are at one with the words, the character and the action. I was thrilled to be acting again. I realized how much I loved my profession. I had nearly forgotten how much, what a ham I was.

Unspoken, subtle signs also told me I was back again in the business. There was a minor stir over my makeup my first day on the set. The head man in Hollywood thought I was wearing too much. I felt my makeup was right for Carrie Louise, my character. I have played many parts without lipstick or any eye makeup, when I felt it was right for a character. I had argued this point with the bosses at Warners not just for years, but over decades. I looked around that first day and noticed none of the women in the cast was wearing any makeup. During the next few days, one by one, they arrived for work in eye shadow, lipstick, eyeliner, blush—the works. And they all looked so much better.

By the time I had finished my two good scenes with Miss Hayes, and adjusted to the pace, I had a ball. I overheard people saying complimentary things about me to Kathryn, and I discovered that I liked it. I had been away from that for what seemed an eternity.

Not many months before, I had attended a cocktail party in Hollywood, announcing a motion picture starring Jimmy Stewart and Carol Burnett. Many of the guests were clearly uncertain what my condition was. There had been stories about my illnesses, but little mention of my recovery. The result was that many of them acted as though they were seeing a ghost. It was as if they had given me up for lost, and at first no one would come near me. The hostess kept asking me to please sit down, as if I did not have the strength to stand.

In effect, *Murder with Mirrors* was my return to the world of the living. Weeks after we finished shooting, I received a letter from Miss Hayes, saying that she wished she had worked with me from the beginning of the film. She had learned so much from me, she said, about how to be comfortable on a motion picture set. She was writing, I think, as a trouper, not an artist, and I take her words as a high compliment. Her achievements on the stage do not have to be repeated here. And as long ago as 1932, she starred with Gary Cooper in the original film version of *A Farewell to Arms*. But movies are a different world, and they have not been her world.

As a gift for Miss Hayes, Kath and I found an antique silver-backed mirror which I had engraved: H.H. FROM B.D. She loved it. She said she would keep it in the powder room of her home in Nyack, New York.

From the moment I accepted the offer to appear in *Murder with Mirrors*, I dreamed of the day Kath and I would celebrate the completion of the film. There was no celebration. I was denied a final victory because of the news I received by phone from New York two days before the end of the picture. I was told that B.D. had written a book about me and not, rumor had it, a kind book. My beloved B.D., whom sometimes I loved over and beyond my love of my work. It was impossible for me to believe. Even now, having read it, it is just as impossible for me to believe.

Though robbed of our celebration by this news, the fact that I had successfully finished my first film after having all those illnesses was a celebration in itself. As Kath so often assured me, we would, we did "make it." Once more I had been given proof that one's work is always what one can rely on.

Not long ago I was asked to go to Paris to receive the César, the French version of the Oscar. I was also decorated by the French government's minister of culture for my contribution to the arts. Kath, who now lives in Paris, did a fabulous job making all the arrangements for my appearances. That night, after the ceremony, Kath and I had every reason to celebrate. And indeed we did!

Dear Hyman,

You ended your book with a letter to me. I have decided to do the same.

There is no doubt you have a great potential as a writer of fiction. You have always been a great storyteller. I have often, lo these many years, said to you, "B.D., that is not the way it was. You are imagining things."

Many of the scenes in your book I have played on the screen. It could be you have confused the "me" on the screen with the "me" who is your mother.

I have violent objections to your quotes of mine regarding actors I have worked with. For the most part, you have cruelly misquoted me. Ustinov I was thrilled to work with and I had great admiration of him as a person and as an actor. You have stated correctly my reactions to working with Faye Dunaway. She was a most exasperating costar. But to quote me as having said Sir Laurence Olivier was not a good actor is most certainly one of the figments of your imagination. Few actors have ever reached the towering heights of his performances.

You constantly inform people that you wrote this book to help me understand you and your way of life better. Your goal was not reached. I am now utterly confused as to who you are or what your way of life is.

The sum total of your having written this book is a glaring lack of loyalty and thanks for the very privileged life I feel you have been given.

In one of your many interviews while publicizing your book, you said if you sell your book to TV you feel Glenda Jackson should play *me*. I would hope you would be courteous enough to ask me to play myself.

I have much to quarrel about in your book. I choose to ignore most of it. But *not* the pathetic creature you claim I have been because of the fact that I didn't play Scarlett in *Gone With the Wind*. I could have, but turned it down. Mr. Selznick attempted to get permission from my boss, Jack Warner, to borrow Errol Flynn and Bette Davis to play Rhett Butler and Scarlett. I refused because I felt Errol was not good casting for Rhett. At that time only Clark Gable was right. Therefore, dear Hyman, send me not back to Tara, rather send me back to Witch Way, our home on the beautiful coast of Maine where once lived a beautiful human being by the name of B.D., not Hyman.

As you ended your letter in *My Mother's Keeper*—it's up to you now, Ruth Elizabeth—I am ending my letter to you the same way: It's up to you now, Hyman.

Ruth Elizabeth

P.S. I hope someday I will understand the title *My Mother's Keeper*. If it refers to money, if my memory serves me right, I've been your keeper all these many years. I am continuing to do so, as my name has made your book about me a success.

198

AFTERWORD

May 12, 1985

Dear Bette,

When I was a little girl living in Madrid for the filming of *John Paul Jones*, you took me along with B.D. to Toledo for the day. I have never forgotten your generosity and kindness to me on that trip and as I watched the two of you all day I thought how loving and committed and *"present"* you were in B.D.'s life. Years later when I visited your hotel room in Egypt (*Death on the Nile*), I saw you had put all these framed photographs of all sizes—heavy ones, not practical to pack—around your room and you spoke a little of B.D. and Ashley, and once again, after all these years, I was struck by the depth of your commitment to your family.

Now if any one of my kids (I now have eight) were to list just some of my shortcomings (as only they could) it would fill a *shelf* of books. I know how heartbroken and outraged you must feel. I'm positive every parent who hears anything about this will feel outrage too, and profound sympathy.

I send you my best thoughts and my love always.

Mia [Farrow]

B.D. Hyman
% William Morrow & Co., Inc.
105 Madison Avenue
New York, New York 10016

Congratulations, B.D. Hyman. Well done.

I have just read your book. I even bought a copy.

You have indeed excelled in what you set out to do; cash in on the fame of your mother.

However, if it is merely the result of your newfound religion, then God help Christianity! Is this why you were born again? Is this what gentle Jesus told you to do?—to hurt, maim, humiliate and mentally crucify your own mother?

Your jacket blurb reads that you write with understanding and humor. I did not find it funny. I found it vicious and with malice aforethought.

How many more times could you describe her whimpering, whining, yelling, screaming or bellowing?

But your writing also reveals your selfish "me" religion; as in method acting, it is all wrapped up in "self" and full of self-indulgence. "Look at me; I have found myself, i.e., God look at me, I'm OK Jack, but my mother is a sinner: she got divorced, she drinks, and smokes and swears."

And why not, might I ask?

Your mother is a great lady. She is a great actress. She has balls and is entitled.

I too am an actress of the old school, and precisely her age. A

202

mutual friend, David Hartman, once told me that she and I have much in common, and I was flattered indeed since I am unknown.

But I too smoke like a chimney. I drink and get pissed; most good actors do. And my language would make a sailor blush.

Thank you so much, David, for getting this letter to me and getting permission for me to use it in my book if I wanted to. The writer wished to remain nameless and I'm respecting her wish.

Letters to the Editor
People Weekly
Time & Life Building
Rockefeller Center
New York, New York 10020-1393

Dear Editor,

So the actress known as "Mother Goddam" in her professional life uses foul language in her private life? What a surprise! And she also tears apart cooked chicken with her bare hands when the knife is dull? Shocking. And at 73 years of age she sends an obstreperous 4 year old to his room for misbehaving? What a witch! And she even has the bad taste to want to avoid a heaven which accepts people who write without a jot of "Christian charity." People who are incidentally sunning themselves in the Bahamas on their "thirty pieces of silver" while their subject fights for her life. I don't want to go to their heaven either. I want to go where ever it is Bette Davis ends up because it'll be a helluva lot of fun and it will damn well have some character to it, you can be sure of that. Not that her daughter would recognize it if she tripped over it.

By the way, I don't remember Bette Davis ever promising

her audience that she would be a helluva mother . . . just a helluvan actress . . . and that she delivered. Anything else isn't really any of our business, is it?

If you know how to reach Miss Davis . . . please forward this to her.

Sincerely,
Elaine Melson Madsen

The Sunday Post, Bridgeport, Connecticut
June 9, 1985—Film Clips by Joe Meyers

B.D. vs. Mommie Bette—Kiss-and-Tell Just Reads "Dumb"

For all of the media buzz over B.D. Hyman's memoir of her life with mother Bette Davis, *My Mother's Keeper* (Morrow) is a pathetically unrevealing book.

When rumors of the book began leaking out several months ago, columnists speculated that the tome was going to be a *Mommie Dearest*–style scandalfest about another beloved superstar. Detroit-based gossip columnist Shirley Eder was so incensed by the idea that she announced it would never be named in her column (which, of course, made for great advance PR).

Unlike Christina Crawford's catalog of genuine horrors, B.D. Hyman has filled 348 pages with some of the silliest and most mundane examples of child abuse that have ever been committed to print. Based on the "evidence" in this book, Hyman's case against Bette Davis would be thrown out of any court in the land.

Hyman gives us a few anecdotes involving heavy drinking, a second-hand account of one of her children getting a severe spanking from the actress, and story after story showing unrestrained bossiness and egomania on the part of Davis. I doubt that this behavior is unusual in most families, let alone the high-pressured world of Hollywood stardom.

Like so many familial mudslingers, Hyman tries to paint herself a passive victim of her mother. Rather than generate sympathy, however, it makes her look dumb. Despite years of exposure to this alleged beast of a mother, Hyman keeps sending her own children into their granny's arms and we've got to wonder why she does it.

In the case of her son Ashley, she agrees to let him make a television movie called *Family Reunion* with his grandmother, which meant working and living with her for several months, thousands of miles away from his parents. If Davis was as bad a mother and as whacked out as Hyman claims, why did she permit her son to do this? And why does she then pretend to be so surprised when it turns out to be a bad experience for Ashley?

The scene which supposedly precipitated the final break between mother and daughter is entirely unbelievable. She once again drops her two kids off to be babysat by Davis—even though her younger child screams out of fear—and then feigns shock at the end of the evening when Justin tells her he was spanked three times by his grandmother. Hyman announces to her son, "Justin, you have my word. You'll never have to visit your grandmother again. I'm sorry for what happened but I can't explain it . . . please don't ask me to."

Hyman rails hysterically at Bette Davis in the manner of someone who has just started psychoanalysis and wants to blame her mother for all of her own neurotic behavior. The book verges on parody in the section in which Hyman attacks her mother for passing off Stouffer's frozen macaroni as a home-cooked dish (the woman includes a step-by-step description of Davis' deception—I kid you not!).

In the closing portion of her book, Hyman very sanctimoniously tells us that she only wrote *My Mother's Keeper* as a last ditch effort to re-open real lines of communication with her mother. What a crock! The author has gone so far out of her way to embarrass her mother that it's impossible to believe this assertion. She quotes Bette Davis making nasty cracks about many of her colleagues and friends in a manner that is obviously designed to get the star in trouble with many other celebrities (these jabs have nothing whatever to do with the mother-daughter focus of the book).

Hyman's case is not helped by the appalling level of the writing. *My Mother's Keeper* is full of poor grammar (which reads like unedited transcripts of tape recordings) and ridiculous attempts to give us quoted dialogue that the writer couldn't possibly have remembered in this detail. Unless the pre-pubescent B.D. was wired for sound there is no way the long quotes could be accurate.

My Mother's Keeper is one of the most squalid and pointless entries yet in the burgeoning Hollywood kiss-and-tell genre.

Keep This "Keeper" Out of Here, Please

My Mother's Keeper
by B.D. Hyman
William Morrow & Co., $17.95.

by Ed Baker, *The Seattle Times*

The condescension of this book's title foreshadows what you find inside: a description of a wildly imperfect mother by a daughter who evidently is flawless.

According to B.D. Hyman, Bette Davis is a nasty-tongued, self-centered harridan who has drunk an ocean of booze and alienated a legion of relatives and acquaintances. Hyman's thesis seems to be that the fighting spirit that helped her mother scramble to the top of the movie-actress mountain also led her to make a mess of her private life. Davis, according to Hyman, has never let kindness or logic interfere with the chance to sting a husband or a child or a grandchild.

Readers looking for insights on Davis' acting career can forget it. The focus of this book stays on its subject's off-camera flaws, à la *Mommie Dearest*.

But *My Mother's Keeper* lacks an exposition of the sort of bizarre traits that Joan Crawford supposedly possessed. While Hyman's report depicts an imperfect woman, some readers might react by saying, "So what?" Aren't there a few other imperfect mothers in the world? And do we expect (or want) a movie queen to behave like a well-adjusted suburban housewife (assuming there is such a creature)?

There must be some redeeming value to this book. A new literary talent? Alas, no; Hyman's writing style slogs around in the true-confessions mire. How about making a few bucks for its author? Alas, yes—that seems to be happening.

Epilog to *My Mother's Keeper:* B.D. Hyman gives Bette Davis a final chance to shape up—to become the kind of mother and grandmother Hyman wants her to be.

Epilog to review: Shut up, B.D.